Facing Life
Head On

Healing with Courage, Gratitude, and Attitude

Carey Portell

Facing Life Head On
Healing with Courage, Gratitude, and Attitude
Carey Portell
Thrive Big

Published by Thrive Big, St. Louis, MO

Editor: Cheryl Roberts

Proofreader: Kay Clark Uhles

Cover and Interior design: Davis Creative, DavisCreative.com

Library of Congress Cataloging-in-Publication Data

Library of Congress Control Number: 2021903154

Carey Portell

Facing Life Head On: Healing with Courage, Gratitude, and Attitude

ISBN: 978-1-7366777-0-4 (paperback)
        978-1-7366777-1-1 (ebook)

Subject headings:
1. OCC011020 BODY, MIND & SPIRIT / Healing / Prayer & Spiritual 2 REL012070 RELIGION / Christian Living / Personal Growth 3. SEL021000 SELF-HELP / Motivational & Inspirational

2021

Acknowledgments

In memory of my friend, Kim, who was the catalyst for me to "Just finish the damn book."

Thank you to my parents for raising me to "get back in the saddle" many times over.

Thank you to my friend, Jen, for reading and editing my first draft.

Thank you to the two best surgeons a broken woman could have and to the endless hospital staff who cared for me while recovering.

Thank you to the emergency crews who cared for me on the scene and at each hospital we were transported to.

Thank you to Davis Creative for giving me a safe place to share my story and referring me to my editor, Cheryl, and marketing guide, Rebecca.

Thank you to Amy Shafer for giving me a last minute title suggestion that is perfect.

Thank you to my community for strongly urging me to share my story.

Thank you to my husband, my life coach, who granted me the time, space, and never-ending support to not only heal but to get these words on paper.

Dedication

This book is dedicated to *you*. *You* are my family, friends, acquaintances, even strangers that took time to help me through this whole experience. *You* held me in your thoughts and prayers. *You*—my family—put your lives on hold until I could function on my own. *You*—my children—practiced patience, were nurturing and learned a lot about independence, while my mind, body, and spirit were reclaimed. *You*, my husband, were my guiding light and best motivator.

There were times when my own light diminished and was rekindled by a spark sent by one of *you*, whether you knew it or not. It was at the oddest junctures that a short note from someone revitalized my ambition to survive and live, the way I wanted to live. I will never be afraid of saying a prayer or sending a message to someone because of awkwardness.

It is said that "If you were not grateful for what you had before, you will never be grateful for what you are about to get." I believe this to be true. I do not wish this experience on anyone; it is painful in so many ways. I am grateful to have lived thirty-five years as I did, but I am grateful to live any way I can now.

If there were a way that I could touch *you,* to transfer my appreciation so you could understand what is in my heart, *you* would be comforted by endless peace. That is how much I am grateful. Gratitude is an attitude! I hold that truth and promise to you that I will pay it forward till the end of my life here on this earth.

Contents

Acknowledgments iii

Dedication v

Preface viii

Chapter 1: The Nightmare 1

Chapter 2: After Shock 17

Chapter 3: Courage 29

Chapter 4: Gratitude 45

Chapter 5: Determination 69

Chapter 6: Easter Mass 87

Chapter 7: Resolve 93

Chapter 8: Believe 101

Chapter 9: Seriously? 105

Chapter 10: Attitude 113

Epilogue 121

Preface

Before we left the hospital for the first time, my amazing husband gave me a journal he bought in the hospital gift shop. He wanted me to have it to take home with me, something to provide an outlet for all I was experiencing. At a time when I felt my life was confused and complicated, I couldn't imagine ever being able to write about what I had experienced or would be experiencing.

Still, as I held the journal, I was transformed. Not only by his attentiveness and thoughtfulness, but its symbolic hopefulness. What we were living through needed to be captured and shared.

It has been ten years since the collision. Unlike the demolition of metal from my collision, my skin and bones, spirit and life were not destroyed. That gift of a journal became my vehicle for healing, carrying me through the worst of times, always with my husband and family at my side.

May my words become vehicles of hope for everyone who reads this book.

Chapter 1

The Nightmare

*I need to concentrate not so much on
what needs to be changed in the world, as on
what needs to be changed in me and in my attitudes.*

– based on *Alcoholics Anonymous, The Big Book*

A truck, popping over a small hill, rounding the corner, careening toward us. I watched as its cab leaned around the curve, its tires not even touching the pavement as it crossed the center line. It was flying, literally flying! Landing in our lane, I saw the truck whipping back and forth across the yellow lines. Back and forth, fishtailing out of control.

"Good Lord," I shout. "It isn't going to stop!"

Panic coursed through my entire body, creating violent tremors. I screamed! It was all happening so fast!

"No!" my mind insisted. "No!" My eyes widened with terror, confusion, and disbelief as huge white lights filled my vision.

"It is too close!" I screamed! I screamed so hard my chest nearly burst from the effort. "Oh my God!" Darkness.

"No," I cried aloud, waking myself up.

My eyes darted back and forth. I felt my anguished heart pounding, a war drum beating inside my chest up into my throat.

It was the nightmare. Again. How many times had I dreamt the same three seconds on this one night? Fifty, at least. Every time I dreamed about the crash, my body reacted as it did that night, and my subconscious mind forced me to relive the impact.

Feeling the sweat-soaked sheets beneath me, wadded up in my clenched fists, I forced myself to gather my wits and recover from the terrifying dream. I brought my hands to my chest, trembling fingertips wiping at the sweat that had pooled on the surface of my skin.

I began saying my mantra out loud so I could hear it. "I know where I am. I know I am okay. I know it was a dream."

Slowly, my darting eyes began to focus. I inhaled and exhaled deeply, repeating my mantra, breathing, until twenty minutes later I felt myself drifting into a slumber, but I was afraid I would be thrown back into the nightmare. I was so tired.

I stared at the ceiling. I looked over at my husband, desperate to wake him, but he was sleeping soundly. Slowing my breathing to avoid hyperventilating, I verbally revisited reality.

"It's been three months," I whispered. "We were hit by a drunk driver. We are all okay. We survived the crash."

I had never had nightmares before, certainly not one that was an instant replay of my real life. That night, lying in a sweat-soaked bed, staring alternately at the ceiling and my sleeping husband, I decided it was time to stop replaying that freezing cold, dark-filled terror.

"Enough," I said. "I'm done. I have to be done with this nightmare."

—|—

Sharing my journey has been emotionally exhausting. Through the first year of recovery and rehabilitation, I focused on a goal of moving forward from the collision. By allowing myself to dive into the details of my trauma, I was able to purge and heal emotionally. I did not push the event to the sidelines. The only way to get over the trauma was to work through it. I could not stop or change what had happened to us, but I could concentrate on improving my quality of life. I had survived a terrible crash. My life was not the same as it was before.

When thinking about the outline for this story, I realized that most non-fiction literature gives a vague overview of the survivor's day-to-day perspective. Few give the reader the intimate details that can be overlooked but are pivotal for recovery. Furthermore, without capturing the details, I wouldn't have been able to convey the humor I and my family experienced while I was recuperating from trauma. Humor is there, but it requires being open and positive. It is a rejuvenating medicine—an all-natural product. I decided to include both humor and details in this story.

Here I was, thirty-five years old, performing tasks (or having tasks performed for me) with and by my husband that we had imagined we might have to do when we were well into our elder years. Shaking our heads and chuckling at several real-life scenes, no matter how devastating or embarrassing, seemed relevant to the story. Elements that appeared trivial would transform into critical setbacks or major accomplishments. I didn't pay attention to "elements" before they became part of my healing. As memories filled in, details revealed simple moments that permitted me to be aware of my blessings. This awareness not only guides my future choices but also rewards me with a positive understanding of what has come from this entire experience.

—|—

Greg and I have a true love story and that's not just my biased opinion. We fell hard for each other at a time when I had no desire to look in a man's direction. A friend of mine kept urging me to meet this friend of hers and I wouldn't think about it until one evening she said, "Well, if you want to see what he looks like, he's right over there."

Well, shit. Damned if "Cowboy Greg," as I began to call him, was a hottie. Later that evening our eyes locked and I was hit by a title wave. I tore my gaze away from his and refused to look his direction for the rest of the night because, remember, I didn't want anything to do with the male species.

Months flew by. You know how it is when you can't get someone out of your mind, right? I was still feeling the sting of Cupid's arrow sticking me right in the ass as we had some unexpected encounters when Greg had been spending time learning to team rope (two people, mounted on horses, rope and immobilize a full-grown Corriente steer) with my dad and brother. It was obvious he was interested, but he wasn't pulling the trigger on asking me out. Yep, you guessed it. I asked him out instead.

It's difficult to describe that our early relationship was a whirlwind romance yet had a calm and stable foundation, but that is how it felt. Greg has expressed to me that he felt we had stumbled along an agonizing broken road to find each other, both having made the most difficult decision of our lives; that is, to leave our first marriages.

I didn't understand what I had been yearning for until I met Greg. Having him in my life as a true partner who offered unconditional love and support gave me the feeling that God sent him to me. He was the missing piece that allowed me to explore the real me. He never keeps count or expects anything in return except to love him back with every bit of fervor as he loves me. And by the way, he said "I love you" first.

Greg and I combined our families in late 2005 after seriously discussing how we would do so. We realized immediately that we were on the same page in how to raise "our family," not "his and mine." We had procrastinated and waited to get married until 2009, just a year prior to the car crash because our lives were beautifully chaotic caring for our one active family.

Greg has two girls from his previous marriage: Hayley and Mackenzie. Olivia and Drew are my children, also from my previous marriage. Our children are close in age with Hayley being the eldest, then Olivia, Mackenzie, and Drew.

We had the normal struggles of blending our families, as most others encounter going through the same thing. Learning to live and share with new people, a blended family, had our children fighting and loving each other as any normal siblings would. Now, when Greg and I hear our children say "my sister or my brother" our hearts burst with love and relief that they have accepted and love each other. Our children were the ages of thirteen, twelve, ten and eight when our lives were altered by the crash. We had been busy in our day-to-day activities. But coming to a screaming halt took the breath right out of our lungs.

My day commenced somewhere between five and five-thirty a.m. each day. I rose early to either prepare breakfast or to create a meal for our dinner that evening. It was the end of the year, and I was in the process of making career changes. I was closing my full-time photography studio and re-entering the healthcare field as an MRI technologist. I had spent the past year in college classes to achieve this new path. My hours at the imaging center concluded at five-thirty each evening, followed by a thirty-minute drive home.

Before I picked which direction I would travel, I checked my schedule to make certain how many and which children I was transferring or gathering from activities. When I arrived at our farm, I hoped one of our children had remembered to cook the dinner I had made that morning and that they had eaten it before we migrated to our next destination. If I were lucky, I could grab a forkful of food before vanishing again, but more commonly the kids would be standing in the drive watching for my truck to appear. One child would call out "Shotgun" before leaping into the front seat. Another would pretend to affectionately "hug" the other. Once we were on our way back to town, I would then realize that picking up my husband's dry cleaning had slipped my mind; a child would call from home alleging we needed milk or they would perish; and another confessed that he had forgotten to give me a note three days ago stating that he needed to bring a snack for nineteen students to school, by tomorrow! Arriving back home around eight-thirty, one of our daughters would broadcast with teenage exaggeration that she needed specific gym clothes or her uniform washed to wear the next school day.

Even though our lives were busy, my husband and I would rush by each other in the hallways, moving from task to task. We would pat one another on the rump and shout encouragement that each was "doing a great job" and to "keep up the good work." The night would end with straightening the house, reviewing the last few photography orders I had, and contemplating my schedule for the next day.

I thought it reasonable that I should be able to add one fun activity into the week for myself and that was to teach a Zumba class, which meant Greg would have to leave his workplace on time to make the hour drive home to cover my duties. Or I had to make other arrangements. He also had to complete the farm chores and any remaining office work to prepare for his early morning meetings.

Sometimes, I would stop and stare, as if I were in slow motion, observing life whirling around me. Our family showed affection often, but our hugs were rushed, unless it was a moment when one enveloped the other in a bear hug and smothered the other's face in kisses before racing out the door. Thoughts of slowing it down would often meander around in my mind, never completely leaving my thoughts. My career changes would help me in my quest to walk a little slower, breathe a little deeper, and capture the quality time with my family I desired. I needed to make this happen so we could be less chaotic, but still successful, in the upcoming year."

I enjoyed my life. As crazy and hectic as every day was, I still enjoyed it. I was smiling as I was speeding past all of life's beautiful events, but I was moving so fast that I could not hear the silence. I heard a lot of voices, even my own, when I stopped to listen. I looked forward to a time when I could rest and be with my family, without cutting it short. I wanted desperately to sit on my couch, in my own house and do nothing but bask in the silliness of the kindred souls I call my family.

I believe that, since I could not accomplish this myself, a greater presence than I stepped in and took control of my floundering attempt.

I should have been more specific in what I wished for.

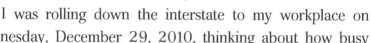

I was rolling down the interstate to my workplace on Wednesday, December 29, 2010, thinking about how busy this day was going to be. I did not realize that this day would be different from any other I had ever known, that it would be etched in my family's memory forever.

Acting as a Zumba instructor in a neighboring town, it was my evening to teach. I used my lunch time at the imaging center to practice my moves for class. Having the television on for background noise, a reality show caught my attention. The show was relating true stories of collisions and strange occurrences. While I sat at our little round table with my dance notes in front of me, I wondered what it would be like if I knew in a few short hours what events were to unfold. If I could not stop the event, what would I do? We have all heard stories of victims that had premonitions prior to some tragedy in their lives. Little did I know that evening, I was going to be that victim.

Looking back at that moment during my lunch break and those thoughts, I cannot help but wonder if it was a message and I was too busy in my life to hear it.

Typically, I drove straight to class, but my husband, Greg, was home with our four children the week between Christmas and New Year's. Wanting to ease his hypersensitivity of the anarchy four children can concoct, I had enough time to run in, change, designate which two children would go with me, and depart in order to arrive at the dance studio by six forty-five p.m. I appointed Olivia and Mackenzie, our two middle children, to accompany me on the Zumba adventure and to help if any of the dancers needed a babysitter while in class. Since the dance studio is a straight shot from the south outer road, I took that route instead of the interstate, as accustomed. I also opted to make our expedition to town driving the car instead of our F350 truck.

Everything that happens in life is the result of a choice. I did not choose to have devastation brought upon me, but I had made three out-of-the-ordinary choices that inevitably led to the events that would change my life indefinitely. It just so happened that another individual was making different choices that nightfall, as well. I believe God gives our souls the freedom of choice, but could fate have assisted in our paths literally crossing that dreadful evening?

The three of us were heading to town and the girls were giggling about how the women shake during Zumba dance. Our classes were of all ages. The girls thought it funny I taught "old ladies" to move like that. We were having a good time, paying no attention to the freezing, dark night as the laughter echoed inside our car.

I glanced to my right. Kenzie, with her signature ponytail at the front of her head, was busting a move in her seat. Olivia's grin was reflected in the rear-view mirror, as she sat behind me in the back seat. We were all three snickering like schoolgirls. Still smiling, as I peered back at the road ahead, my grin diminished as I was trying to accept what was happening before my own eyes. My lips parted in astonishment. Blood stopped flowing through my veins and my lungs refused to push air out of my body.

I said, whispering it incredulously to myself, "It's on the wrong side of the highway."

"What?" one of the girls asked, confused. I could not respond. I didn't want either girl to look at what was unfolding before us.

A vehicle, a full-size pickup truck, popped over a small hill, rounded the corner ahead, careening toward us. I watched as its body leaned into the curve, barely able to keep its traction, going so fast. It crossed the centerline into our lane, and for a moment it seemed to be flying, its tires not touching the road, then it hit the asphalt and started fishtailing out of control, back and forth across the yellow lines.

"Is this really going to happen? To us?" I shouted in my head for it to get back to the other side of the road, but it barreled towards us like a freight train.

"Good Lord," I screamed. "It's not going to stop." It was happening so fast! My eyes were anchored on the vehicle. "Going too fast. No!" My mind roared. "No! It's too close." In a split second, headlights were glowing in my face, filling my side window, blinding me. The white headlights were all I could see!

I jerked our car to the right trying to avoid the imminent crash.

"Oh My God!" I screamed into the white lights as the truck whipped off the end of the trailer in front of us, smashing head on into our car.

The truck pivoted, crashing into my driver's side door. There was a horrible crunching of metal, shattering plastic, our vehicles, spiraling, twisting into the dark night.

My legs were crushed from two directions, pushed off to the right, metal puncturing my skin, piercing my lower legs. I did not hear my bones exploding into splintered bits, some exposed, protruding out of my skin. The second impact launched my body against the center console, splitting my pelvis and ripping small bones from my lower vertebrae. The harmless controls of my dashboard ate away at the skin on my hands as they were raked back and forth like a rag doll. Tissue tore in my left shoulder as the truck caved in the door on my left side.

Later, I learned that Olivia had tucked her head between her knees and covered herself with her arms as broken glass tumbled over her bent body in the back seat; that my studio camera, which had been sitting beside her in the back seat, had launched with such force that it fractured her right wrist; and that Mackenzie was jerked violently that her seat belt lacerated her lower right abdomen.

When our car was hit, nine air bags burst open to cushion the blow from momentum and mass of the other vehicle. The collision was so intense that pieces of our car were catapulted in every direction, filling the sky with falling debris. Any part of our bodies that were not restrained were brutally flung in all directions. Our skin was scraped everywhere, with deep dark bruising appearing instantly. And that was the good news.

Bones! So many of my bones were broken. Darkness took me into its arms as soon as we were hit, shielding me from the agony that just kept coming as our car caved around and into my body, but not before I accepted that I was going to die. Not before I begged God to take me and save our girls.

The phenomenon of "having your life flash before your eyes" in near-death experiences did not happen to me. I had no time for that. There wasn't a moment to reflect on the past or the future. In a tenth of a second, my brain was trying to accept what was about to occur. I was desperately trying to figure out how to avoid what was happening, and I begged, I begged with everything I had in me, for God to save the girls' lives.

Six-thirty p.m. I started to wake just like the actors do in the movies, trying to lift my eyelids, feeling as if they had weights hanging from them. I was conscious that my blinking was slow. My mind was foggy. I couldn't focus. I had no idea where I was or what had happened. Finally, I was able to stop blinking and focus my eyes. Why was I looking through the driver's side window at grass? It was at the level of my window or my window was at the level of the grass, and I could only see it in black and white.

When our car stopped spinning after the impact, we were in a ditch alongside railroad tracks. Our vehicle had crashed into some pine trees and was now facing in the opposite direction I had been originally driving. Our safety belts had kept us from being hurled out of our seats.

I was trying to make sense of what I was seeing when I heard what I thought were people yelling at me. Where was that coming from? Did I hear "Mommy?" It had to be the girls. They were both calling my name, begging me, "Please wake up, please! Talk to us!"

They demanded to know, "Are you okay?" Words were penetrating my muddled mind.

"Mommy, I think I broke my arm," Olivia said.

Broke her arm? What was she talking about? Then it started coming back to me, creeping through my confusion. Dear God, we were in a collision! I knew it had to be terrible. There was no way we could have been unharmed after a crash like that.

Olivia's voice was trembling as she stated again, "Mommy, I think I broke my arm." I turned my head toward her voice, but my movement seemed delayed. When I turned my head to the right, there was only darkness with a white light in the upper left corner of my vision. Why couldn't I see them? I knew my eyes were open, I had just been looking at grass.

I tried to give them reassurance, but I couldn't get the words that were in my head to reach my lips. I spoke to them. "Calm down. People will be here to help us soon. Call 911."

Partial words were coming out, but they understood enough to act. Olivia grabbed her cell phone from her pocket and called for emergency help. Again, I tried to move, to help the girls, but I still could not see them. Something was pressing on my chest, preventing me from turning in either direction. The lower half of my body wouldn't move. I was trapped.

"Why can't I feel my body?" I whispered. There were shadows that kept trying to wrap around me, breathing down my neck. I fought for consciousness.

I heard Mackenzie say in a small voice, "Carey, I think I'm cut on my belly pretty bad."

My heart sank as I wondered what injuries they had sustained. My little angels were hurting.

"Can you see the cut, Kenzie?"

She then stated confidently, "No, no, I think it's okay." Then mere moments later, the worry is back in her voice as she whimpered, "No, Carey, I think it's pretty bad."

To hear her tone—the way she was dramatic one moment, then nonchalant the next, it was just so Mackenzie. I don't know how humor could show up at that moment, but it did. Even though my heart was aching for the girls, it let me know her personality was still intact. I had heard them both talk and their speech was coherent, which was a comfort. They didn't have brain damage. I did not hold this same confidence for myself.

"Call Greg," I instructed the girls.

Olivia said, "A woman took my phone to finish the 911 call."

"My phone is in my purse," I whispered.

Mackenzie asked with all her sassiness, "Where the heck is that?" Again, a small smile.

"It was on your floorboard before the collision."

"I've got it," she reported.

I was so proud of these two girls. They were so calm.

Olivia called Greg. "We are somewhere past the big rocking chair," she told him. "Come now."

It had been about eight minutes since we left the house.

I had so many thoughts inside of my head, but I couldn't get them to form into words that would come out of my mouth. Worried about how badly the girls were injured, frustrated that I could not move, I wanted to hold each of them tightly and whisper comforting words in their ears. They had to be frightened. I must have hit my head because I could not stay focused on what was happening. Greg must be frantic wondering why Olivia called instead of me. He must know this is something awful.

I heard Olivia ending her phone call with Greg, and I tried to turn toward her voice once again. That small movement released the most God-awful, intense pain I have ever felt. It hit me in my lower legs. Like an explosion. Overpowering. I didn't know such pain existed. Sensation had indeed come back to my body. I wanted it to go away. It was too severe. There was no measure for this on a pain scale. I reached down and could feel that my legs were pinned. Debris surrounded them. Sharp metal poked into my muscle and bone. I thought that if I could move them, even a little, maybe the horrendous agony would stop, but the slightest movement made my body convulse with pain. I rested my forehead on whatever piece of the car was against my chest and decided to try a second time. Pulling a little harder, I was hit by waves of nausea and let the darkness take me into unconsciousness.

There is pain that makes us cry. Then there is pain that makes us vomit. Finally, there is pain that is so severe our body's natural response is to send us into shock. It is intolerable. The body shifts into survival mode. I entered this last phase, gratefully.

Chapter 2

After Shock

Nothing, absolutely nothing happens in this world by mistake.

– based on *Alcoholics Anonymous, The Big Book*

I was unaware of people surrounding our car, helping keep all of us calm while we waited for the emergency crew to come to our aid.

I listened as the paramedics began to remove the girls from our demolished car, then I floated in and out of consciousness for the remainder of the lengthy extraction. Confident that Greg would comfort the girls, I gave in to the darkness waiting to claim me. Firemen and paramedics continuously woke me with questions. Yes or no answers were all that I could mutter. My normal temperament is to stay calm, and I seemed to be staying true to my nature. As was customary, I waited quietly and answered when spoken to.

Greg was not allowed to come to my side of the car when he arrived. When they finally called him over, he kneeled so he could speak through my window.

"Carey? How are you doing?" he asked.

The sound of his voice made my resolve to stay strong shatter. "It hurts so bad," I whimpered, but no tears could come. I was in shock. I could see an outline of him, but every part of me felt his presence. I could tell him the truth, that I hurt worse than anything I could ever have imagined, and I wasn't sure how long I could take it.

I remember little of the extraction. I do remember looking out my window, my gaze landing on Greg and my dad standing by the railroad tracks. My vision was in color again. They had their hands shoved deep in their pockets and they stared at me with solemn faces. Anguish for them consumed me.

I tried to reassure them I was fine and not to worry, that I was grateful they were both there, but they did not respond. I assumed I had not actually spoken the words. I was speaking novels in my head, but the words were not emerging past my lips. I tried to show emotion through my eyes, but by this point I was incapable of accomplishing even that. I was afraid I had the empty stare that I had seen on the faces of collision victims I had taken care of while working in the x-ray department at the hospital. I hated that they had to see that hollow, in-shock look on the face of someone they loved. I let my eyelids fall shut so I did not have to witness their heartache.

During this time, Greg watched Mackenzie be taken from our car and loaded into the ambulance on a gurney. She had sustained a deep laceration to her lower abdomen from her seat belt. She complained of extreme soreness over her chest and her right collar bone where the seat belt left its mark on her. The paramedics needed to start an IV, unsure of how severe her trauma could be. Mackenzie and needles do not get along, at all. Nightmares would plague her young mind for months.

Greg carried Olivia to the ambulance and sat her beside her sister. Her bare feet were cold. She'd had to remove her boots that were filled with sharp, broken shards of glass. She was sure her left lower leg was broken, but she didn't notice her right wrist was in pain as well.

Olivia asked the emergency crew over and over again, "How is my mom? Is she going to be okay?" but the paramedics had little information on my situation as I was still trapped in the car. Mackenzie was having a difficult time as the shock was wearing off and anxiety set it. Olivia grasped her hand and told her sister, "We just need to pray, Kenz, everything will be okay."

In the midst of cutting the car apart, one of the firemen instructed me, "Carey, we are going to have to remove the roof of your car to be able to get you out. You just sit tight."

"Okay," I acknowledged. "Greg's gonna like that!" I exclaimed in my head. Humor again cutting through the seriousness of our situation.

I believe the healthcare training I had received helped me understand the phases I was going through and how I needed to respond. I also was consoled at the thought that at least one person among the emergency crew would know me personally.

During the extraction, there was always a paramedic to the right of me in the car, soothing me, quieting any fears I had. Since my husband was unable to be near me, it was essential for someone else to be there for support. He was firm and direct when asking me questions or disclosing what action they were taking next. Consoling and supportive, professional and compassionate, I will be forever grateful for each and every one of the emergency-care workers and their demeanor as a team.

After the roof was removed, Greg leaned over the hood of the car and told me, "The ambulance is leaving, Carey. It's taking the girls to the hospital in Rolla, but they have to fly you to Barnes Hospital in St. Louis. What do you want me to do?"

"The girls cannot be alone! You go with them, take care of them." I said the words while my mind panicked, knowing how difficult this would be for him.

Greg already knew this is what he needed to do; he knew this is what I would want him to do, but he asked me anyway. "Your dad will stay with you. You won't be alone, and he will give me updates on you until I know the girls will be all right. I'll come as quickly as I can."

I was comforted at the thought that Dad was going to be there with me; but at the same time, I felt such angst for Greg having to watch his family being separated from each other, taken to two hospitals in different directions. He was being forced into a decision to leave me, not knowing how severe my injuries were or if we would ever speak again. I could feel his angst and his incredible strength. All this heartache because of this impaired driver's decision to get behind the wheel.

I remember nothing else until they slid me into the ambulance. Immediately, paramedics cut off my clothes; and when the woman had to lift my right leg, I could not help but moan in pain. As the scissors slid up my abdomen to my chest, I cringed. Instead of donning a sports bra, I had stuffed shoulder pads into the shelf bra of my tank top before leaving my house. I privately snickered, imagining the paramedic's confused face if one of those pads fell out. The next thing I vaguely remember was the "Emergency Room" sign as I was being wheeled into the hospital in Sullivan, Missouri. I remember nothing while they performed CTs and multiple x-rays of most of my body.

Then my dad was at my bedside and he asked me, "How are you doing, Carey?"

My resolve shattered twice in a matter of hours. There are two people that I do not have to be strong for, two people that I can let see me at my most vulnerable: my dad and my husband. I sighed inside, relieved that I could tell him how I felt.

"Daddy, I broke both of my legs," I whimpered in an almost childlike voice, reverting to a childhood endearment in my most exposed moment.

"They are getting ready to transfer you, Carey. Greg is with Olivia and Mackenzie at the emergency room in Rolla. He'll meet us at Barnes as soon as the girls are released."

"Olivia and Kenzie?" I asked.

"The girls are injured but are going to be just fine. I am going to call Greg and let him know they are moving you on to St. Louis now."

He called Greg, telling him, "She does not have brain damage or organ injuries. It's a miracle. Her bone damage is severe, but she will survive."

Then I was being pushed back into another ambulance. The female paramedic apologized. Leaning near my ear, I could hear the compassion in her voice as she told me, "Carey, we need to move you to another hospital. We can't fly you because it is too foggy. I'm so sorry, but we have to drive to Barnes Hospital, and it's going to be a rough ride."

Moaning, I begged, "I don't care. *Please* just give me some pain medicine so I can go to sleep."

Gratefully, I have no recollection of that ride to St. Louis.

As I traveled the highway to the city, the girls were being assessed in the emergency room themselves. Olivia and Mackenzie were separated as soon as they arrived. Olivia was worried, asking about her younger sister multiple times. Mackenzie was having a CT on her abdomen to determine how much damage the seat-belt laceration had caused. Fortunately, it could be sewn up with twenty sutures and she would heal. Olivia's right wrist was throbbing uncontrollably by the time she arrived at the hospital; and after x-rays, it was determined her wrist was broken but her left leg was fine. Olivia was wheeled to reconnect with Mackenzie, and they spoke of how sore their bodies were. They were soon released and Greg headed toward me.

Prior to driving to the crash scene, Greg instructed Hayley not to tell Drew anything about the crash until he figured out what had happened and how badly we were hurt. Hayley had heard her Dad's side of his conversation with her sister, Olivia, and this had her stomach churning, wondering if her family was going to be okay. When she and her brother, Drew, were picked up from our house by my mother-in-law, Hayley told Drew that we had been in a bad car wreck and we were hurt but she didn't know how badly yet. Tears trickled down her little brother's cheeks until they began flowing like a waterfall. They sat holding each other for hours. Months later, Drew and I were speaking about that night and he whispered to me, "Mom, when I heard Hayley say all of you were hurt, I didn't want to believe it. It felt like a dream and my heart stopped."

Hayley had stayed strong for her brother; but when she was able to reunite with her sister Mackenzie, all the pent-up emotion she had been holding in exploded to the surface and demanded to be released.

Being wheeled into Barnes-Jewish emergency room mimicked a scene from a television drama. Nursing staff immediately surrounded my gurney, throwing out questions to me and the paramedics.

A male nurse leaned down and said, "Rate your pain on a scale of one to ten."

At that specific moment in time, my pain seemed to have decreased. Also, my foggy mind figured that if I said ten, well, that would have meant it was the worst pain of my entire life and might imply that I was weak.

I said, "Six."

His voice changed to humorous as he flatly stated, "Yeah, right."

Clearly, I was delirious. This was the worst pain of my entire life.

As I was being examined and taken to radiology, Greg arrived, along with my family and his best friend. He watched as I went through a barrage of procedures. Every part of my body had an injury from the impact, which required every part of my body to be examined.

My family was informed: "Carey's ankles and pelvis are severely injured, but there's no brain or organ damage. Her worst injuries are to her lower legs. She has a compound fracture of her right ankle and the bones of her lower leg have been crushed. Her left ankle has been broken and drastically dislocated anteriorly, severing nerves as it did so. She also has a left posterior pelvic fracture; two bones in her lower lumbar spine are broken; and she has excessive bruising and scrapes all over her body, especially the lower half."

I was grateful I didn't remember much from after I had entered the ER until I awoke the next morning.

When my eyes opened, I was greeted by two of my friends and their husbands standing at the end of my bed. My immediate response was gleeful, as I had not been able to visit with them for some time, but for the life of me, I couldn't figure out why they were there. Then, out of the corner of my right eye, I saw my dad. As I kept scanning, I found Greg and my uncle sitting beside my bed. "What is going on?" I asked myself silently. To my left I spied a hospital curtain, then, looked down at my legs covered by a light blue hospital blanket.

"Oh God," I thought. "I've been in a car wreck." Last night's events started coming back to me. I floated in and out of a sleepy stupor the rest of that morning. When I was awake, I was filled with questions. I was distressed about the girls and didn't understand why we were taken away from each other. I could not grasp that they weren't in the hospital anymore, that they were released and at home. I didn't even understand that it was the next morning.

"Carey, the girls' injuries weren't as severe as yours, so the ambulance took them to a smaller hospital. That hospital couldn't take care of you because your injuries were too severe," Greg responded. "But they have been released and they are being taken care of by family so I can be here with you." The pain medication had my thoughts and many of the memories from the prior evening scattered and confused.

At one point when I was relatively conscious, I overheard Greg tell my dad he needed some air. I watched his back, shoulders slumped forward, head hanging as he walked away. I didn't know whose injuries hurt the most: my actual but medicated injuries; his unfathomable emotional pain as he was torn apart from the inside out.

Much later, I asked him about that moment. He told me that he had gone to the main level of the hospital and found a seat near the water fountain.

"I was doing okay until I saw two of your friends walk in the corridor and I lost it. I put my head in my hands and wept," he said. "Wave after wave of emotion washed over me and it kept coming. I kept my composure until that exact moment. I knew I had to get you and the girls to a place where you were stable. There were so many phone calls and texts that I had to shut our phones off. I didn't allow myself to think about how close I was to losing you three until that moment. I felt sick."

Greg and I have always been complementary to each other, always by each other's side. Hand in hand, each supporting the other. This was one time he had to carry all the weight on his shoulders.

During my ten-day stay at the hospital, I was taken to the operating room twice and had three surgeries performed on my ankles. An amazing orthopedic trauma surgeon salvaged as many pieces of my broken bones as he could and pieced them back together like a puzzle.

I was distraught with pain while I was in the recovery room after each operation, as witnessed by Greg and my parents. The pain of having my bones manipulated and fastened back in place was more than I could bare. It seems I let everyone know the torment I was in and how unhappy I was about it, crying out for someone to make the agony stop. They had never in their lives witnessed this kind of reaction from me. This shocked me as they relayed it weeks later.

When I came around in my room after one of the surgeries, I am not sure if it was my personality, God, or the medication called "Dilaudid," but I awoke in a great mood. If I received my medicine routinely, I was in moderate pain, light-hearted, and didn't think much about my situation. While I was holding my mom's hand after a surgery, I vividly recall a divine sense of prayer. I spoke genuinely to her, "Mom, I can *feel* everyone praying for me. I can *feel* it. That's why I feel so good. It's as if everyone is holding me, using prayer to carry me over everything that is happening because I cannot carry myself."

It was an inspiring feeling, one that I cherish and will remember forever.

Chapter 3

Courage

Never be ashamed of a scar. It simply means
you were stronger than whatever tried to hurt you.

— Unknown

Olivia and Drew were brought to the hospital by their dad to visit with me. When we caught site of each other, all we could do was smile and hold our arms out to hug one another. I clasped them tightly and never wanted to let go.

"Here you go, Momma." Olivia handed me the small teddy bear that had been mine since I was three years old and that I had given to her when *she* turned three years old. My sweet daughter made sure she was taken to our home from the hospital to retrieve it. That bear had brought her comfort and she wanted to deliver that same comfort to her momma. My heart could have exploded at that moment at her thoughtfulness.

"When do you get your cast?" I asked.

"After the swelling goes down a little, they'll put my cast on." It was her right arm, and she was right-handed, so it would be difficult for her to manage while she healed.

"How's my guy?" I asked Drew. He was eight years old, and he didn't know what to think as he stared at my extremely swollen legs. External fixators had been placed into each of my lower legs. Essentially, six bars were drilled into the bones of each lower leg to keep them in place. I was staring at his awe-struck face as he said, "I brought you a bag of candy. Thank you for staying alive, Mom!" he said as he held it up proudly.

I cherished their visit and I hated to see them leave. Visiting with them and being able to see that they were okay picked up my spirits. But being without our kids made my heart hurt.

Hayley and Mackenzie arrived at my room with solemn faces. They cried immediately upon viewing me lying in the bed. I comforted them as we embraced, and Mackenzie displayed her lower abdomen.

"Look, I have twenty stitches, Carey!" The seatbelt laceration, while painful, would heal, and it was the worst of her injuries. I was so relieved. Our kids are so strong. They don't realize how strong they are, especially at such a young age. I wasn't sure how the girls' injuries were not more severe. I envisioned that God had His arms around us that night. He could not stop the collision from occurring, but He absorbed most of the impact for us.

During those days after my second surgery, there was a moment when Greg and my mom were in the room with me. As I was asking them details about the collision, I had no recollection that there were four vehicles involved. In my mind, I remember two. They broke the news that we were hit by a drunk driver and that he did not survive.

Time froze in that moment. Complete shock encompassed me. The air did not move around me or in my lungs. I could barely hold on to a clear thought anyway, but knowing I was involved in a fatal car crash left me speechless. My mind did not want to take it in. One of my first thoughts as I started coming to after the crash had been wondering if we would all wake up. I had no idea someone *had* died in that fateful moment.

I kept asking questions, sometimes asking the same questions over again because I did not recall asking them the first time or I didn't remember the answer. While I was lost in my own thoughts, I heard Mom say something about my face.

Oh God! I had been consumed with my ankles and had not even considered that I may have lacerations or burns. In fact, I had not even looked at myself above the waist, at least that I could recall. I asked for a mirror and they explained the left side of my face was burned from the airbag. When I viewed my image, I was a little taken aback by the reflection. I scanned my face, and it was red from the burns and my skin was peeling off in some places. There was a perfect line down the center of my face, showing that I turned my head to the right when we were struck.

I examined the rest of my body and discovered it was beaten up. I had bruises everywhere, deep, purple bruises, competing for a spot of skin with cuts and scrapes. My left shoulder had a deep throb where something was torn. I could barely move it.

How my face and upper body were spared from the glass, I still can't figure out. The glass had penetrated once at my hairline and once above my lip. Minor scars for such a severe tragedy.

—|—

The day before I was released, I was jolted to consciousness by an excruciating pain low in my right leg, centered exactly over my crushed fibula. I inhaled sharply and deeply, then held my breath, unable to speak as my face contorted from the anguish.

"What's happening?" Greg asked, moving quickly to my side. "Carey, what is going on?"

I tried to express what was happening, but everything was locked up by the excruciating spasm. It began slowly, warning me to prepare, then it rushed over me with a wave of convulsions. I thought my leg was being shattered all over again.

Greg called for the nurse as I collapsed back to my pillow. I grimaced as my eyes slammed shut. I was gasping for air. There was a traction device over my bed and with the next spasm I grasped the handle and growled as my teeth clenched together furiously. Involuntary, short grunts were coming out between my gritted teeth as I endured the torture. This happened time and time again, never relenting. I had no control over this searing pain. A sob escaped my lips as I was fighting another spasm. I knew I could not take anymore. "Please!" I begged, silently.

"Can you help her?" Greg begged the nurse. Then in a moment I will never forget, Greg sobbed my name as he laid his head on the bed beside me, grasping my right arm. His voice was a kind of vulnerable I had never heard come out of a human being.

My nurse stood to the left of my bed. She looked at me and I saw her tears fall as I fought through the spasms. She frantically called for the physician to obtain permission for an additional dose of Dilaudid. My shrieking did not stop until she pushed the fluid through my IV. Quickly, the spasms subsided and I abandoned consciousness.

—|—

Then came the real fun. A physical therapist taught me how to get out of bed and transfer myself to the wheelchair. We toured the orthopedic floor as I learned to maneuver my new ride in the hospital hallways. When I returned to my room, the nursing staff was as giddy as I was as I succeeded in wheeling myself around. I giggled at the thought that they let me operate it while under the influence of such strong pain meds. Everything was a splendid blur and I was in good spirits. That's when I started seeing the humor in everything.

My nurse entered my room explaining that I could be discharged if I had a bowel movement. She was candidly holding a suppository in her hand.

"Do you want me to insert it or would you prefer to do it yourself?"

My head whipped around to look at her hand. I was bewildered and appalled. She asked so casually, as if this was an everyday occurrence for me.

"Uh, I'll do it," I stammered. Good grief, the things I must go through! I knew anytime there was surgery, or an extended hospital stay, the policy was that patients had to have a bowel movement before they could be released. I just had not thought about it for me. Later, I was abashed when Greg told me that wasn't the first time I had encountered the nurse with a suppository.

I had been in the hospital for ten days and, after a successful BM, I was released to go home.

I remembered one of my favorite quotes by Theodor Seuss Geisel: "When something bad happens to you, you have three choices. You can let it define you, let it destroy you, or you can let it strengthen you."

I vowed to be strong in all things, even suppositories, if not for myself, for my family.

—|—

Dear friends and family helped move me into our house that evening and even borrowed a hospital bed to put in our living room. Vague details of men attempting to remove me from a van plague my recollection. I recall laughter as they didn't know where to place their hands and not cause pain; also, because I was wearing blue paper pants.

Greg was lucky enough to be employed by a company that allowed him to work from home two days a week. My mom and Aunt Bev stayed with me the other three days of the workweek. Greg, the kids, and my dad were with me each evening, and many visitors brought loads of food.

If I even remembered that someone visited, I could recall them as a blurry outline. I made a mental note that the meals were the greatest gift that anyone could have done to help, besides prayer. The meals continued for three months, keeping my family (and likely me) from starvation during my recovery. My husband refused to leave my side to sleep comfortably in our own bed. He slept on the couch beside me for three months, setting his alarm every four hours to administer my medication. Each morning and evening he gave me injections in my abdomen to prevent blood clots. Also, he was instructed to clean the wounds each evening where the steel rods entered my skin from the external fixator on my right leg. He took care of the kids' needs, along with mine, and was thrown into the position of being in control of every aspect of our lives. Figuring out things very quickly, he did it without complaint; but as I lay in our living room recovering, I knew he had to be feeling the stress of it. I also knew he stayed strong so that I would not give up.

Greg and I had agreed on most things in life, rarely arguing. Not to say we haven't had a heated debate that resulted in a few days of silence now and then, but never to the point that we questioned our marriage. Our life is busy but never boring, we aggravate each other just enough to keep things interesting. Most nights when he was trying to find a few hours of sleep to revitalize himself for the next day, I would stare at him. I never knew a relationship could feel like ours. Absolute certainty that we were both giving our marriage everything we had, never having to question one another's love and commitment. The respect and value we both openly granted one another sealed our relationship. Greg and I have a wish for our children, that they see that even though our life and relationship is not perfect, there can be a true-life love with never ending work and devotion.

I slept the first two weeks I was home, but I lay awake every night of the third week. Greg did not sleep much because I did not sleep. Trying to convince him I could take my meds when the alarm erupted was futile. He did not think I was cognizant enough to perform this task.

I lay awake each night and stared at the ceiling, trying to find any comfortable position, any at all. If Greg did doze, my entire focus was to not do anything to wake him. I watched him sleep and thought about how much he meant to me.

Those sleepless nights made me strong in an odd way, as if being able to endure wakefulness, discomfort, and irritable, relentless pain, I could endure anything. My hope was that I could be as strong for Greg as he was being for me.

Personal hygiene took the form of a sponge bath. I thought I should be upset about this, but I was on Oxycontin, so I wasn't too upset about anything. Greg would wheel me to the bathroom, and I would hope I got all the cracks and crevices cleaned, but who knew? A very heavy cast on my left leg restricted my movement, and I could not bend forward enough to reach my toes. I barely skimmed the right leg because of the amount of pain involved. My mom and aunt used a tub and buckets to wash my hair every few days while I lay in bed in the living room. My family made it all work and were wonderful about making compromises with their own lives while I waited for my body to heal. I was as good a patient as I could be, given that I hated being so dependent.

—|—

It was time for my first checkup after surgery, two weeks after being released from the hospital. The pain had been monotonous for the past week. My appointment was at seven-fifty in the morning. We were gifted a hotel room close to the hospital as our drive would have taken nearly an hour and a half to commute.

The night prior to my checkup, I did not sleep, not one wink. It was the most difficult night of my conscious life. I could find no comfort. I knew I needed IV pain medication. Thinking that I would slumber, I waited. Greg and I did everything we could think of. We re-situated my body, re-elevated my legs on pillows, took pain medication. Nothing, absolutely nothing relieved the constant pounding, stabbing, fire that was penetrating my lower legs.

With all my heart, I told Greg, "I am miserable." I bluntly instructed him to move me to the couch so he could get some rest.

When we left for the hospital, the temperature was zero degrees outside, literally zero. The only clothes I could fit over my legs with the rods that were drilled into my bones were flimsy gaucho pants. Greg bundled me up the best he could. At zero degrees, the steel rods in my right leg gave me a whole new meaning of the phrase "chilled to the bone." Barely tolerating the pain as the frozen air traveled up the metal shafts and entered the very core of my broken bones, right then, I wished with all of my might that this would go away. The pain was gruesome.

"I don't want to do this anymore." I told Greg. He looked at me. "I wish that this had never happened. I know it's not going to go away, no matter how many times I wish it would; but right now, I do so wish it had never happened."

"Me too, Carey," he said, lovingly tucking me into the seat.

—|—

Assigning us a disability parking tag had been overlooked, so Greg had to wheel me a greater distance than anticipated to get to the doctors building. The air was frigid and there was ice on the parking lot. It was a huge feat to move me and not create a great deal of pain in the process.

Terrible, crippling anxiety overtook me as I anticipated our journey from the parking garage to the doors leading to the offices. My first anxiety attack, *ever*. It was not dramatic, only Greg and I knew about it. But there I was, terrified of being bumped, dropped, sliding on the ice. I trusted my husband completely, but this feeling of total, helpless fear overpowered me, coursing through my veins.

Greg transferred me from the parking lot to the hospital with skill and calm, as usual, and soon I was calm, fully embracing the warmth of the corridor as it hit my face.

The next thing was the nurse removing the cast and rows of sutures from my left leg. During my hospital stay, I didn't have any sensation when the residents ran their fingers over the toes of my left foot. Now that the cast was off, we realized I did not have any sensation from my ankle down to my toes. It was void of any feeling, numb. The nerves had been torn and severed. Nerves naturally try to reconnect over time. We could hope that the feeling would return, but this was entirely up to my body.

As I was listing my complaints to the surgeon, Greg reminded me, "Don't forget the most important one."

How could I have forgotten? "My pubic bone has been 'popping' for the last week."

"I can hear it," Greg said. "It's like a wallop or clunk. I can feel it pop when I'm carrying her."

My surgeon stopped walking and talking. I didn't like the look on his face. After a few questions, he immediately scheduled me for some x-rays and a CT of my pelvis.

Greg and I returned to the patient room. My surgeon entered, closed the door, and leaned heavily against it, gazing at the floor with a grim expression. It was clear that it was hard for him to tell me.

"Your pelvic fracture has not healed as expected. Normally, this type of fracture fuses itself, but your fracture hasn't fused. You are one of a small percentage that has not followed the textbook."

I knew I would need another surgery on my right leg, but then the surgeon dropped his bomb. "You have to have major surgery on your pelvis. I have to implant two bolts in your left posterior pelvis and a plate and screws on your pubic bone to hold your pelvis together while it heals."

That sounded like torture. I did not want to imagine it. Greg took my hand. We were both devastated. I felt this horrible heaviness, as if an elephant had decided to sit on my chest.

It hurt to breathe, my chest wouldn't expand, forcing me to take shallow breaths.

I did not hear much of what he disclosed after his description of what he had to do. I was still trying to grasp it. I understood three things at that moment. This meant more pain, more scars, and more recovery. I controlled my emotions while he gave us instructions about scheduling the surgeries for the following Tuesday. Then he left the room.

Greg's expression said it all. Total dismay and disappointment. He slowly walked the few steps between us and wrapped his comforting arms around me. He didn't need to say anything. I didn't need to say anything. Everything was conveyed in our loving embrace. The new level of endurance required by this news, along with our continuing situation, was almost too much. As hard as I tried, I could not stop a few tears from seeping through my eyelashes. He gingerly wiped them from my cheek, then treated me to juice and a danish before we left, trying to keep my spirits high, and I'm sure his own, as well.

Our return trip to the truck was exacerbated by the fact that, even though the nursing staff had provided two leg braces when they released me from the hospital, we, did not realize we were supposed to bring one of them with us to my first appointment. Because my left leg was not supported, the discomfort started to take control of my temperament. I was as fidgety as a child in church. Rolling to the car, every crack in the sidewalk caused pain to radiate through that left leg. It felt like a miracle when Greg slid me into the back seat. He had pillows supporting every part of my body and I begged for a pain pill. As it started to alleviate my deep discomfort, I began to drift off to sleep. Greg handled it all so well. Literally every motion was torment for me. My breathing was labored, and I worked to regulate it. It was not easy for him to carry the burden of my pain. There was nothing he could do to take it away. He just had to stay strong.

—|—

By seven that evening, there was considerable stinging radiating from my left foot and ankle, which had been supported for three weeks by a cast, but now had no support. It felt like acid was flowing through my foot and ankle. It kept escalating until it was so intolerable I dialed the after-hours phone number of my surgeon. I did this because I was maxed out on pain meds and my choices were to have Greg drive me to the nearest hospital or wait it out. That waiting it out thing was not going to work.

"Put the brace on," my surgeon suggested. "Your ankle and foot have to form a ninety-degree angle to each other. Your ligaments and tendons are being stretched before they are ready, and your fractures still need constant stability."

It sounded so simple. Put the brace on. Fitting that brace on my leg proved to be one of the hardest tasks Greg and I would have to perform. A thousand theoretical knives were stabbing into the bottom of my foot for three hours.

"Check my toes," I demanded of Greg. "I'm being electrocuted, and I feel as though some of them have blown right off my foot."

"They are all there," he assured me as we tried several times to push my foot farther down into the brace, each time producing unimaginable pain.

"Could this pain be as bad as the torment from the night of the collision?" I asked.

"The night of your collision, you were in shock. It buffered your pain."

Having that information did not help. I could not induce shock and I couldn't endure anymore pain, but I had no choice. I collapsed in Greg's arms and moaned in pain. We were both frustrated and exhausted.

"I've never experienced anything like this. I have always been able to control myself. I'm not one to give up," I told Greg, but I wanted to give up.

He maneuvered pillows until we found a position that seemed to ease the pain a bit. By early morning, the worst of the stinging had subsided. No more acid being injected into my foot and ankle. Finally, I embraced my exhaustion and dozed. It had been a dreadful night for both of us.

I had three days to prepare for my next surgeries, but I wasn't managing very well. I felt nauseated most of the time, and I was experiencing severe vertigo because of having to lie flat for most of the day and night. Oh yes, and then there was the amount of pain medication I was consuming. If someone had not been caring for me, I would not have remembered to eat or even attempt to go to the bathroom. I may have appeared lucid to some visitors, but I was zooming around Looneyville on a red scooter, holding yellow balloons. I had been instructed to transfer myself to the wheelchair at least three times a day. I accomplished this in noticeably shorter increments. My legs had to be elevated and any motion was excruciating. I did not look forward to more surgery, except I knew that while recovering in the hospital, I would slumber like a newborn in her momma's arms. I desperately needed sleep.

Chapter 4

Gratitude

Acceptance is the key to my happiness. When I am disturbed, it is because I find some fact of my life unacceptable to me, and I can find no happiness until I accept that situation as being exactly the way it is supposed to be at this moment.

— based on *Alcoholics Anonymous, The Big Book*

"Seriously, we have to leave our home by three a.m.?" It was a rhetorical question. I knew at three a.m. on Tuesday morning we needed to head to the hospital for my next two surgeries. My husband performed miracles. He did this all the time, but at three a.m. on a cold, dark, why-are-we-even-awake morning, he slid me onto the back seat of the truck, which was lined with blankets and pillows to cushion me for the long ride.

"I'm going to lock up. I'll be right back." He hurried back into the house to lock all of the doors and grab our belongings.

At that moment, anxiety coursed through my body again. It flowed from my fingertips, up through my arms and legs and settled in the center of my chest.

"Okay," I told myself, "I'm nervous about this surgery. It's harder. I know how terrible I'm going to feel recovering from it."

Saying it out loud didn't seem to reduce the pressure on my chest. "Is it because I'm alone here? I need Greg. He'll calm me down." Then I realized, I did not want to burden Greg.

"God will not carry your load unless you ask him to," I told myself, tears rolling down my cheeks. Without thinking about it, I turned to Him. I closed my eyes, rested my head against the pillows, and with more sincerity than I had ever felt before, I said, "I'm having a hard time. I need You to help me."

It was that simple. At once, the hammering in my chest stopped, and I knew with complete certainty that I was going to come through this surgery just fine.

"You okay?" Greg asked after coming back from locking up.

"Yes," I said, knowing that what had calmed me would be with me forever.

—|—

When Greg and I entered the pre-op room, some of the surgical staff recognized us. I was confused because I remembered no one! Greg laughed as he reminded me how feeble-minded I had been from the amount of anesthesia and pain meds I'd had recently.

It seemed like a minute later that I was consciously lifting my eyelids, aware that I was leaving the operating room, moving beneath huge lights and passing through a doorway. Nursing staff were wheeling me to recovery. Instantly, an awful pain began to radiate from my pelvis. Within moments it was unbearable. I asked the nurse where I was and why I was feeling so much pain. I did not remember any of this from the previous surgeries.

A male nurse said, "You are at Barnes Hospital. You are not supposed to be awake yet."

I did not believe him. My teeth were chattering violently. I had no control over my body as I began to shake. He asked me if I was cold or if I was in pain. I told him it was horrible pain and asked him to make it stop. As soon as we made it to recovery, I was given morphine, but the pain would not subside.

This wasn't different from the other surgeries, except this time I was conscious. The nursing staff could not give me anymore morphine because it slowed my heart to four beats per minute. Morphine was not working. Finally transferred to the orthopedic floor, I was injected with Dilaudid and slept. Waking up every so often, I could feel my face was grimaced with pain. It was odd that I could feel this, but I couldn't do anything about it. The pain meds had taken away my ability to move or talk, but I could grimace. And I could find relief in an uneasy slumber.

Greg and I were blessed with wonderful nurses during our hospital visits. There was one nurse that stood out. She had been with us during most of our stays.

"Hi," she whispered in my right ear. "When I saw you were on the surgery schedule, I asked to be your nurse."

My eyes were still closed, but I knew her voice. I wasn't sure if my smile made it to my face, but I was so delighted. She had made our stay comfortable under trying circumstances. She was especially helpful for Greg since, the first time around, he stayed in the hospital with me the entire ten days. She was impressive, smooth, and sociable. It was clear to me: Nursing was her destiny. She possessed the most important qualities and they radiated from her core.

There's no way to communicate the importance of having such an amazing person there, caring for me and my husband, in the very worst of times. I will be forever grateful for her.

—|—

It was the last morning of my stay. I was excited until the physical therapist (PT) announced, "You have to start rolling to each side if you want to leave the hospital."

I cannot describe how badly I did not want to do this. I was in anguish, lying flat on the bed, trying NOT to move.

"You do not have a choice." He made it clear that I must roll.

It took several nurses and the PT to roll me to my left side, positioning pillows and pulling up sheets.

Greg was dozing in a bed next to me when my uncontrollable, horrible involuntary groans woke him up.

"What's going on?" he asked.

"My muscles are being torn from my pelvic bones," I groaned. I asked, inside my head, just how much more pain was I going to have to endure. I wanted to sob and tell them to leave me alone!

"Great job, Carey!" They were patting me. "You did really well. We will be back in a few hours to roll you to the right side."

"Okay, thank you." I was so polite to my tormentors.

The right-side movement was not as terrible as the left roll. I was feeling pretty good until I learned what my next feat was to be.

"Now you have to sit up."

This would surely kill me. I didn't say it out loud, but I was thinking pretty angrily, "Are you kidding me?" If looks could kill. The PT snickered and told me, "You can do it."

I knew I could do it. I just didn't want to! She was patient as I moved at a slug's pace. It was absurd how difficult this was. Sitting up, she let me rest a mere moment before exclaiming, "Okay, now into the wheelchair!"

For the love of Pete. smack me with a two-by-four and put me out of my misery! I knew, of course, I had to move or I would not be leaving. I also realized she was correct when she told me, the more I moved the easier it would be. Okay, I obliged. I kept thinking, "Soon I'll be home. It's time to go home."

At home, my existence was confined to the living room. This meant my entire life was set out for everyone to view. Moving to our bedroom was unacceptable until I could get in the bed. I have always enjoyed my privacy and independence. It was challenging to be so openly, though lovingly, observed; and it was against my nature to let everyone take care of me. I knew supervision was a necessity due to my physical limitations and mind-altering medications. And although I am unbelievably grateful to everyone who adjusted their schedules to accommodate me, I needed to be able to stop for a moment and reflect on the eight weeks that had passed.

When my mom leaned down to kiss me goodbye one evening, I told her I did not want her to come take care of me anymore. I had come to the decision that I needed to spend some of my days alone, to reflect on what had happened and how my life was now unfolding. I needed to cry. I needed to sit in quiet. I needed to talk with God and to myself. I needed to know that I could get my own plate and fix my own lunch. I craved independence. She had tears rolling down her cheeks. I thought she was crying because I had hurt her feelings, but she said how proud she was of me that I wanted to begin the journey of taking care of myself.

It had been eight weeks since the collision. The pain medications had kept me from displaying my many emotions—the feelings of despair, thoughts creeping into my mind, anxiety ripping into my chest as if someone gripped my heart in their hands. I was never alone during these moments, so in an odd way, I couldn't fully experience them. I didn't want to inflict them on other people. There was a circus of thoughts, performing all day in my head, making dramatic appearances and I needed to sort through them.

Here's the thing. So far, I had not asked myself, or anyone else, that one question: "Why did this happen to *me?*" There was no reason. I had no control over whether the crash happened or not. It's not as if I could go back in time and change things, right? So why dwell over it? What I *was* frustrated with was the pain and the amount of time it was taking for my mind and body to heal.

I spent the next few weeks mastering the wheelchair and learning to retrieve items that were out of reach. I realized there were still many activities I could do while sitting. I had to be creative about how to accomplish them.

I knew that if I sustained a can-do attitude that would give all of us the strength we needed to get through these difficult times. I might not be able to stand up, but I could still give adversity a swift kick in the butt. There was no room in my recovery for self-pity or excuses. I've never cared for excuses. I am all about goals. Applying my nature to my situation, I could win.

—|—

I was supposed to feel good about the brutal tingling and muscle spasms coming from my left foot. My surgeon said that these meant the nerves were trying to reattach to each other. If those feelings ceased, that meant the damage was too severe and I would have no feeling from my ankle to the toes of my left foot. Consequently, each time I felt like my toes were exploding, I reminded myself that "it was a good thing!"

All of these sensations made me develop an unusual interest in how my body functioned—separate from my perception of how it was functioning. My toes felt as if they were crossing over each other or as if someone was pushing up on the ball of my foot. I would literally lift the covers off to see what's going on, but I saw nothing. Everything was as it should be, except my mind and my body were not able to communicate correctly. I was experiencing sensations that were not occurring. This continued twenty-four hours a day, never releasing its hold on me. Members of my family were now accustomed to my groans as my nerves contracted into random spasms, unintentional gasps escaping from my lips.

I believe suffering is not a punishment—it is a result. My suffering was the result of another person's choices. I couldn't change what had happened, but the kind of person I am is a matter of my character, not my circumstances.

At my post-op visit, my surgeon explained I could start movement in my left ankle, but it would be another three months before I could move my right ankle. Greg and I ran through the timeline. We realized, yet again, how extended my recovery would be. We also realized I would not be going back to work. Greg expressed that we should concentrate on my recovery and not what this meant for our finances, but we were both disappointed.

I believe the same questions were floundering around in his thoughts, just as they were in mine. How were we going to live? Eat? Pay bills? Medical bills in the amounts of ten, twenty and even forty thousand dollars had started arriving. Our lives had been turned upside down in an instant. On top of it all, I had received confirmation that my right thumb was fractured, probably from being slammed into the dash of the car. It had already begun to heal itself, so we left it alone. It was so very minor compared to the other injuries.

I began living Newton's Third Law—*Every action has an equal and opposite reaction.* As pain started to ease a bit, extreme vertigo and nausea plagued me. It was partly from the plethora of pain meds I was taking every two hours, but it was also due to lying flat for most of my day. I was not eating due to the nausea; therefore, I would try to lengthen the time between pills, until the pain would rip through my body and force me to swallow them. Feeling as though a hole was being ripped into the lining of my stomach, I dry-heaved constantly. If I lifted my head, dizziness immediately forced me to put it back down. This vicious cycle continued for over two weeks before I couldn't tolerate any more. I did not care if I had pain. I could not put another pill with codeine in my body.

My body had become dependent on the Oxycontin and Percocet; and even though they were replaced by another medicine, when I quit them cold turkey, I started having withdrawals. Jittery shaking started in my limbs, then I had "the sweats" and could not control my irritable moods. It felt like I had restless leg syndrome throughout my entire body. In my mind, I had been proactive, telling myself as soon as I could stand it, I needed to stop the narcotics, but they took hold so quickly.

Luckily for me, they made me terribly ill, which counteracted the desire to continue taking them. Within a few days, the shaking stopped and sometime later my moods improved, slowly returning to normal. Regrettably, not before I hurt my daughter's feelings, snapping at Olivia for a reason that I could not recall thirty seconds after I had said it. I will never forget her wounded expression. It made no difference that I didn't mean it or that it was the narcotics talking—once words are out, they are irretrievable. For me, it was and will remain inexcusable. I still apologize and hope that time will heal that moment for us both.

—|—

"I'm tired of having the living room as a bedroom," I declared one evening. "I want to sleep beside my husband. I'm tired of my entire life being out in the open for everyone to view."

Greg looked at me.

"Please?" I begged.

"Okay, let me see what I can do." Greg made every accommodation he could think of.

"When did our bed get so high?" I asked as he lifted me onto the mattress.

Being able to be beside each other, lying there, was so comforting; I was able to fall asleep. Two short hours later, my body announced it was too soon to have made this change. It felt as if I was sleeping on a bed of concrete. After conforming to the shape of a wheelchair for so long, my body resisted lying flat, even with pillows under my legs.

I wanted Greg to move me back to the living room, but this was also the first night he had slept in our bed. Judging by the snoring that was bouncing off our bedroom walls, he seemed to be enjoying his slumber, so I did not wake him.

After dozing off around four a.m., I had another dream about the collision.

I was panicked and my heart was racing. Hearing people calling for me with urgency in their voices made me search for them, but no faces emerged. My legs would not come free of the debris, my surroundings were dark. I turned to my left and pushed against the back of my driver's seat. My right hand reaching high into the air, hoping I would feel a hand confidently grasp mine, trying to reach the voices. "I'm here, please help me! I can't get out!" I called. Darkness everywhere. I kept calling so they could find me. Their voices continued to penetrate the emptiness but still no faces.

Awaking with a jolt, I found myself in my bed and not my annihilated car. My position in my bed was exactly as it had been in my dream. My weight was on my bent left knee, my right leg straight out to my side, jerking towards my chest to free it from the debris. My left hand was resting on the headboard as it was on the car seat in the nightmare, and my right arm was straight up in the air, my hand reaching for somebody, anybody to grab it.

My breathing was deep and labored.

"Carey are you okay?" Greg asked.

"Babe, I couldn't get out of the car, my legs were trapped. I pulled and pulled, but I couldn't get out."

"Your legs were jerking and that's when I woke up, come here." Greg pulled me towards him.

"I couldn't see anyone, Greg, and I was reaching as far as I could possibly reach." I said as my breathing slowed.

My cowboy put his arm around me and stroked the hair at my temple until my breathing was slow and deep as I began to rest again.

The dark, terror-filled nightmare, repeating again and again. Monstrous headlights, glaring through my side window, in my face, turning my face into a hideous open-mouthed howl. The moment approached before I screamed for our lives and then complete darkness. My heart pounded out of my chest as I used the nightmare to revisit and judge our fate. It was as if

I had been hit all over again. I wanted to sob. At some point I fell asleep. Again.

Recanting my terrible night to Greg the next morning was difficult. My chest felt like it was being ripped open from the memory of it.

He was sympathetic, compassionate, and, as always, patient. He understood how real it seemed to me, as he frequently had vivid dreams of his own. I had started my emotional journey and chose this time to find the words to express what I was feeling to Greg.

"I need to talk about that night, all of it. It all happened too fast. I have such scattered thoughts and emotions about myself and the girls. Thoughts of you." I asked, "Can you talk about it with me?"

He communicated the specifics of the night to help me piece it together. It was painful for me to watch as he relived it, unearthing the heartache, visualizing flashbacks of the scene.

"When Olivia called me, I answered, 'What's up, sis?' I thought you guys had forgotten something because you had just left. She told me you were in an accident and that all of you were hurt.

"I told Hayley that I would have someone come to the house but not to tell Drew until I found out how bad the crash was. It was when I was driving down our driveway that I wondered why you didn't call me, and then I got worried. I skidded to a stop behind an emergency vehicle. I ran past the first two demolished vehicles, but I didn't see them. I was focused on our car. The passenger side was what I saw first and I thought,

'Okay, maybe this isn't so bad.' I spoke with the girls first because your side of the car was filled with firemen trying to get you free. The paramedics didn't want Mackenzie to move; they didn't know how deep her laceration went into her abdomen. I talked to her while they transferred her from the front seat to a gurney, then to the back of the ambulance. Olivia climbed out of her window in the back seat but couldn't walk because of the broken glass in her boots. I carried her to the ambulance, took off her boots, and set her beside Kenzie. A fireman told me I could come over and talk to you.

"Carey, when I saw your side of the car…I closed my eyes. My heart sank. I asked how you were doing and told you about the girls leaving in the ambulance. The most difficult thing I have ever done was to see how broken you were and to leave you trapped in that car. It tore my heart to pieces.

"I called our parents to let them know what hospitals the three of you were being taken to, and I had your dad stay with you and call me with updates. When I knew the girls were taken care of, I called Jason (Greg's best friend) to meet me at Barnes Hospital and then it was a waiting game while the doctors assessed what kind of damage you had."

It took a long time and all his willpower to give me the details I needed so badly, but he talked until I was satisfied. Greg said he could go over the events of that night in this type of detail once and only once. We were both emotionally exhausted from reliving the details by the time he finished.

I have been touched deeply by the events of this disaster. Life had been extraordinarily simple and, for me, remarkably clear in its purpose. Now, my priorities were being redefined, my spirit touched. That last discussion about Greg having to choose who to go with was a big one. I can't imagine how difficult it had to be for him at that moment in time.

Once the journey of remembering started, sorting through my emotions became an all-consuming trial. Instead of taking one day at a time, there were occasions when an hour was excruciating to battle through. I was struggling with pain, sorrow, and questions about my future. I kept thinking about what *could* have happened and asking why it hadn't.

My life had come to a complete halt. The three of us were spared, which is not the usual result with a drunk-driving collision. I was thinking about it relentlessly, wanting to know the reasons we were granted life and he was not.

"What is it I am supposed to do on this earth?" I drove myself crazy with this question. I did not purposely decide to dwell on it; but like my nightmare, it crept into my mind during the countless hours I spent in bed. The blocked passage to my grief had been ripped opened and all I could do was submit to the flow, as if I were caught up with all the debris flooding through a broken dam. All I could do now was let things come, accept what I could, and measure what I had learned from the experiences. Moving forward was my only option.

—|—

The winter of 2010-2011 did not want to end. Fiercely needing springtime air and sunshine, I began to roll myself out my front door to perch myself on the wheelchair ramp my family had built for me. I watched traffic speed by on our rural highway. I watched the clouds float in the sky. I watched birds pick at the yard. I spent countless hours loving on my Australian Shepherd, Callie. Crisp edges still tinged the air, but the warmth from the sun's rays gradually warmed my skin. After being cooped up in the house for months, I felt compelled to spend as much time outside as possible.

Feeling the sun on my face, I let it wash over me. I had never been so grateful to feel the warmth from the sun's rays in my life.

I was completely at peace and grateful to be alive. Feeling acceptance for every single aspect of my life completed me. My life would never be what it was. It was changing, and it was up to me to be there as my own coach and cheerleader.

Accomplishments made their appearances slowly. Figuring out how to retrieve a plate or cup on my own without standing was interesting. Most days a member of my family would lay these items out for me, but mornings with four kids can be quite hectic. Who is excited about doing laundry? "No one," says every mom in America. I was, though. Able to set the basket on my lap and wheel to the laundry room gave me satisfaction that I could be at least a little more independent, and I wanted to decrease the load placed on Greg's shoulders.

With small changes, the time came when I was ready to cleanse not just our clothes, but my whole being, my personality. I was starting from scratch with my life. Gifted with a strong need to voice how much I love the people who are close to me, I was also able to grant and ask forgiveness from others.

During that time, I experienced deep conversations with some of the people in my life, wrote letters to others, and smothered Greg and the kids with "I love you!" daily. All this brought me closer to satisfying different, newly defined needs.

Trying to describe to Greg how deeply this event had touched me was difficult. He hadn't experienced the same things I had experienced. Although sympathetic, I could see in his eyes that he wasn't able to fully understand all that I told him about this emotional and physical roller-coaster ride. Expecting him to do so would have been unfair of me.

This tragedy had damaged me in unimaginable ways; and even while my spirit had grown, my body continued to define my focus on life. During a particularly emotional discussion with Greg one evening, I was chest deep in purging my feelings about why I was left on this earth. An unexplainable flash of heat overcame me. Resting in my wheelchair, facing Greg, who was sitting on the couch, my head in my hands, tears on my cheeks, I exclaimed, "Good grief, is it hot in here?" I could visibly see the realization wash over his face while mine held a look of bewilderment.

"Don't you remember that you are in premature menopause?" he inquired.

My jaw fell, my eyes opened wide. Shocked and appalled, I said in my most demanding voice, "Are you *serious*, Greg? How fair is that?" I challenged.

He nodded as a smile tugged at the corners of his mouth, bursting into a full-blown grin.

"It's not fair," he agreed. "For you. Or for me, either."

I realized how much he had been enduring, more even than I knew. And then we laughed. Out of all the memories I have lost, this is one that is carved into my consciousness. I choose to believe it stayed to remind me that there is humor in every situation if we are open to it.

Our children always stated they were doing fine when we would ask how they were coping. We were constantly being told how resilient kids are by friends and family, but we knew this situation was difficult. I was worried about them, whether they were getting enough attention from us. Were we asking them enough questions regarding their feelings? So much concentration had been on me and my injuries that I wanted to ensure they did not feel forgotten. Along with the intensity of our new normal, the kids were entering into a highly hormonal phase of their lives. Things can get dramatic, and perspectives can be quite different when hormones are out of balance. I would catch myself becoming too motherly at times. Struggling with the realization that half of our family had come so close to death, I caught myself smothering them at a time when they wanted to be left alone.

As the warmer weather advanced toward us, I continued slipping outside at every opportunity. I was able to roll down the ramp to the sidewalk and start pulling out the dead foliage in the narrow flower bed. New growth was beginning to emerge from the soil, just as it was within me.

Years earlier, the garage had been converted to my photography studio; the computer was in there as well. Desperate for an opportunity to communicate with the outside world, I negotiated with myself to roll to the outside door and enter. Easy enough, right? I placed my chariot at the short incline that led to the door. Then releasing the brakes, I pushed the rubber wheels in a forward motion with too much exertion. The next moment I was tipping backwards and looking at white clouds in a baby blue sky! My first of many wheelchair accidents.

Lifting my head off the concrete pad, I raised my legs high in the air. The force of the fall then hurled me out of my seat to the left, knees bent to my chest. My body stopped on its left side facing our back pasture, staring at a startled, wide-eyed cow across the fence. Dumbstruck, I remained there until I could check my body parts for injury.

Okay, all seemed to be in order.

Turning to my right, I again took hold of my metal chariot, which was still lying on its back. I pulled it across the hard surface, got it upright.

It struck me. I am alone. Outside. Unable to walk or use my legs in any way.

"Didn't really think this through, did you, Carey?" I asked out loud.

Positioning my blue rig directly behind me, I set the brakes to the locked position and placed my hands on the seat. I began to push myself up. I was so afraid the chair was going to fall toward me with the weight of my body leaning on the front of it. Every movement was killing me. My muscles had atrophied. There was no strength in my arms; I could not use my legs to push myself up to my seat. It took me four times, hoisting, heaving, giving myself pep talks while I was praying, before I was able to get back in that seat. Heavy breathing battered my lungs and my skin was coated with sweat.

"Well, that was stupid!" I told myself—again, out loud.

Resting there, it seemed to me the garage door was smirking at me. Yep, of course I tried again.

Rolling to the door, I swung it open and placed a hand on each side of the frame to pull myself up and over the threshold. The wind chose that time to suck the door closed directly onto my fingertips. Wailing expletives, I hurtled myself and my wheelchair to the interior of the garage, then laid my head in my hands. My lower lip was sticking out so far I could have rolled right over it on my way to the computer. After the crash, there were times when life became overly dramatic for me and this was one of those moments.

Situated at the computer, I scrolled through the abundant emails in my inbox while my fingers throbbed from the door being slammed on them. Deep aches started emerging from my bones as I sat there. After all that effort, the pain from my tumble and exhaustion from getting into the garage, I could not respond to those messages. I was overcome with emotion, not from the tumble or the pain but from the tremendous amount of support expressed in those emails. I felt the power of being loved by a community of people. I was overwhelmed. I couldn't reply yet. Not today.

On my way out of the garage, in an unladylike fashion, I boldly flipped off the garage door with my unmanicured middle finger, then rolled back to the front of the house. I made my way to the bed in the living room, settled myself into the usual position, placed ice packs on my ankles, and popped a pain pill to ward off the expected misery I'd inflicted upon myself. I then formulated a conversation that I would have with my husband, Cowboy Greg, when he arrived home from work.

—|—

"So here's what I did today," I told Greg when he arrived home that evening from work. I spared no detail about my humiliation and ultimate success.

"You're a big girl," Greg told me. "And while you can make your own decisions about what you do to care for yourself, maybe you should be more careful next time."

"Agreed," I said.

I was moody. Three months had passed since our collision. Having decreased my narcotic dose, I was more lucid, which meant I was experiencing more of my daily pain. Misery was normal. Moodiness came from lowering my narcotic consumption and frustration from not being able to accomplish what I wanted to do each day. I had never sat so much in my life.

My mind would not allow me the focus I needed to read. I stared at the television without seeing or hearing it. Exhausted from all my healing, I was bored and didn't like not being able to drive or leave my house on my own. I felt helpless.

Then I got pissed. Dependency is not part of my personality.

I told Greg one night about how frustrated I was feeling.

"Do you realize this is at least the third time you have hit this wall?" he asked me.

"No!" I said, remembering this time only. What do I do? I don't go around the house screaming or throwing things, but it was clear my family could sense how irritable I was.

"How you feel and react affects our entire family. It affects how I respond at work and to our kids. Your grief is our grief. It's difficult watching you go through this; and when you are struggling this hard, it is heavy on our shoulders. No, you are not lashing out, but we can feel your frustration," Greg confessed.

Exactly what I was afraid of.

"And I thought I was hiding it so well!" I told him sarcastically. "I don't want to talk. I don't want to be alone, yet I don't want to be around anyone. I want to stand up!"

"We are all in limbo, Carey. We don't know if you will ever walk well again. We don't know if your ankles will hold you up. We don't know how long the actual healing is going to take. We don't know much, except," and he looked at me so lovingly, "you are surviving. We are surviving!"

Reminding me of this helped. I was grateful to be alive. I was grateful we were all still alive and surviving.

"I don't want to give up on the life God granted me. Somehow, I will work through this and learn patience. I promise you I will. Please, God, grant me patience because this is more difficult than I could have imagined."

"We'll do this together," Greg affirmed.

We then talked at length about how I could find peace with dependency until I could do things on my own. I could see it was wearing on him. He'd gotten upset once, at least that's all that I can remember, and I believe I was the one that pushed his buttons. Understanding that I did not know what I was saying most of the time required great understanding from him. He was a living angel. His patience, understanding, thick skin, and love for me carried all of us. I held onto his strength so tightly, I hoped I did not drain it from him completely.

Thoughts of how fully I was going to recover were constantly boring their way into my mind. I wanted Greg to understand my thoughts, feelings, all of these emotions swirling around inside of me. He was compassionate, but I saw in his deep brown eyes, he had his own struggles to deal with.

He couldn't understand because he was experiencing a different side of this tragedy. It wasn't fair of me to get upset, but I was at my lowest, saddest point in recovery. If it hurt so terribly to sit, how much more excruciating was it going to be to stand.

"Maybe it would be better to stay in the wheelchair," I said without believing it. "Maybe it would be better to remove my right lower leg. Anything had to be better than what I'm going through, what *we* are going through."

"You're recovering from more than broken bones," he reminded me. "You're coming off major medications, going through an early menopause, having to depend on everyone else for almost everything. You deserve to be pissed."

"But why do I feel so abandoned? Why do I feel alone at times?"

Greg held my hands loosely in his. He looked tenderly at me, "Carey, you are asking me why you feel alone during your weakest moments?"

"Yes," I admitted.

"I think this is your answer." He then read aloud a quote that he had seen in the hospital gift shop:

"Why, during my hardest times was there only one set of foot-prints in the sand?"

God answered, "You were not alone. That is when I was carrying you, when you were not strong enough to carry yourself."[1]

I stared, awestruck at him, lips parted, eyes wide with understanding. I could not believe how true those words rang. Greg's timing with that story was impeccable. I sat there and allowed it all to sink in.

"I admire you so much," I said.

He knelt on the floor beside my wheelchair and caressed my hand. "I can't fix this part for you, Carey," he said, sympathetically. "It's clear you have a difficult time accepting the idea that you are vulnerable and have to depend on others to take care of your needs. You feel guilty and it's causing a great deal of frustration. Let us take care of you. Make yourself a priority for once in your life. I don't just love you, Carey, I adore you."

I'm sobbing by the time he finished.

"Let it all out," he said. "It's time to let it all out."

I sobbed on his shoulder until I could sob no more. My husband carried me to our bed, gingerly laid me down and crawled in beside me. He slept so close to me, never losing touch with my skin. I adore him as much as he adores me.

—|—

---

1 Based on poem, *Footprints in the Sand,* by a currently disputed author

Our society wants instant gratification. Our patience has decreased. I must allow myself enough time to accomplish my goals. Do you know how many times I have heard the phrase, "All in God's time, Carey"?

It was easy to become frustrated by these words. I was the one living it and feeling as if healing was not coming fast enough. How many times had it worked out that way for me in my past, though? It always happened at the time I needed it to happen. I realized it after the fact and was impatient while I waited for it to happen.

It wasn't difficult for me to understand I should continue taking action to heal myself. What was difficult was having to stop pushing my body further than it was capable of at this time.

I repeated to myself, "The key to my sanity and success is acceptance of where I am at this moment in time, and I continue to trust my faith."

Chapter 5

Determination

You were given this life because you are strong enough to live it.

– Ain Eineziz

For three months, I have been lying in this hospital bed in my living room with the same question invading every thought. It's both conscious and unconscious. I have no control over its interference with my life. It was as if someone annoying were poking me in the shoulder every half second. It kept going through my head: "Am I going to be okay?" For three long months this question nagged at my mind as pain invaded my body. I kept begging for the pain to stop, for the question to be answered.

"AM I going to be okay?" *PAIN!* "Am I GOING to be okay?" *PAIN!* "AM I GOING TO BE OKAY?!" ***PAAAA-INN!*** No rest, no reprieve. Maddening!

—|—

The scene was set in black and white. Two separate white lights were casting a triangle of light down towards a concrete floor. One of those lights were above me and the other was on the opposite side of the dark room. My chest felt afraid of what was coming, I didn't know what that was, but I knew it would upset me. A man, dressed in black, slowly stepped into that triangle of light and looked right at me. He looked tired, worn. "I'm sorry," he whispered. "You hurt me." I whispered back. "I'm sorry," he said softly. "You hurt me." My voice cracked as I felt grief constrict my throat. "I'm sorry," softly, again, coming from him. "You hurt me," I sobbed at him. My chest and shoulders heaved from the breakdown of my emotions. Convulsions racked my body as I finally released every single emotion that had been stored up inside of me from staying strong since my pain had begun.

Greg was shaking me, urging me to wake up. He was on his knees, looking down at me with concern dripping from his voice.

"My God, you are sobbing, Carey. What's going on?"

"He came to me and told me he was sorry, and I finally told him, Greg. I told him how much it hurts."

It's some afternoon during the week, not sure which day; it doesn't matter. I lie in this bed, weary of watching television. I cannot focus enough to read; it is painful to write; I am weary of my own thoughts. Closing my eyes, I drift to some meditative state. Still hearing voices from the television, still knowing my surroundings. That blasted question even intrudes my thoughts here. For God's sake, just leave me alone!

Sensations. Odd sensations. I am smiling. With my eyes still closed, a big easy smile spreads across my face. I don't understand it, but I love it. I want more. Warmth slowly washes over me, enveloping every part of my body with gentle calmness. I feel swaddled by it, as a mother would swaddle her infant.

Splendid peace enveloped my body, mind, and spirit. With a trust so unbelievably complete, , I knew the answer to my unending inquiry.

"Yes," I tell myself. "Even if I do not walk well or ever again, I will be fine. If I must live life in a wheelchair, I will be fine. Our girls and I had survived and that is all that I care about. I have my mind, my determination. I'll be fine."

With the heavy weight of not knowing lifted, my heart began, once again, beating in earnest, with hope.

It was this realization that I would be fine that allowed my next revelation. I was in our house, where I had been for months. All motion seemed to have stopped, except for the whirlwind in my mind. Everything around me seemed to get clearer, as I opened up to this new awareness with awe and disbelief.

I figured out how I had found my answer. The man who was responsible for the collision. It was him who let me *feel* my answer. He was the only one who could *give* me my answer. He could let me feel *peace*. It was him, the man who died in the collision.

I sat straight up in bed, exploding with emotion! What happened? Was it real? Then I heard myself talking.

"I am so sorry. I'm so sorry you died. I'm sorry you died and I didn't. I don't know why, I'm just sorry."

I had been struggling with survivor guilt. I didn't know what to call it, but I found the answer for what I had been feeling by researching the web. Finding the terminology, giving it a name, came as both a surprise and relief. Not everyone around me understands why I had these feelings. I had done everything right that evening; the crash was not my fault, but my heart knew a life had been lost and the lives of myself and my children were saved. My heart was struggling with the "why."

I'd never met him or seen his face, so I wasn't able to picture him. I didn't know his life or personality, but I could feel his heart and knew that God granted him the ability to find peace. He was at peace. I felt his peace. Which made it possible for me to be at peace. I didn't know what that meant, but I knew it as well as I know my own name.

I acknowledged that he had changed my life: first with the collision, then for the second time in a matter of three brief months, he changed it again. He was with me, giving himself—this was the day I granted him forgiveness. Not just for him, but for myself, to bring myself peace. I so needed to feel peace.

I know the reality. I know the explanations: *I must have been dreaming. It was the effects of the pain medications. It was my own mind wanting something so badly that I imagined it.*

Does it really matter? I had found what I didn't even know I was searching for. My spirit felt at ease. I was no longer haunted by questions. I did not care how it had come about; I loved what it achieved.

The meaning of faith is having complete trust or confidence in someone or something. I couldn't see faith, but I felt it. It was my choice to believe—and it granted me peace, courage, and composure. I chose to believe.

—|—

It was mid-March. I was pale from never leaving the confines of my home and cabin fever had taken its toll.

"Let's go grocery shopping," Greg suggested. "You ride up front with me, see how it feels."

"Okay," I said.

This seeming small step was huge. It helped us gauge how often I could make trips from home. Transporting me anywhere was a hassle because I was helpless getting into or out of our truck.

He hoisted me onto the seat, as usual, with no complaint. We headed to Cuba, Missouri, twelve minutes from our home. But Greg did not turn left towards the interstate, instead he continued to drive on the outer road. Suddenly, I was aware that my fists were clenched, my heart had stopped. We were driving the exact route of our collision.

Was this an oversight or his way of urging me to overcome this obstacle?

"You passed the turnoff," I mentioned. I was getting nervous.

Instinctively, he reached for my hand, holding, caressing my clammy skin.

"Where was it?" I asked.

Greg said, "Right here."

My eyes moved to the right side of the road. Our wreck happened at night. The scene looked different in the daylight. Railroad tracks, pine trees. "Is this what PTSD feels like?" I thought.

Vague memories created an ache deep within my heart. That night, the impact, our girls' quivering voices all brought a heaviness to my broken soul. I was thrown into a silent, lonely place filled with immense sadness. Painful memories of the chaos chiseled through my protective wall, and I wondered how long it would take for my spirit to heal.

As we passed the spot in mere seconds, quietly, slowly, with long, deep breaths, my body began to release the tension, as if a fever were breaking. Reaching our destination, I let go of Greg's hand and ripped my jacket off. Covered in sweat, I announced, "We made it."

A week later we again headed to Cuba, but this time night had fallen. We were attending a fundraiser my family had organized for us. Before I knew what was happening, I was staring into a huge set of white headlights passing by us. Mesmerized by their intensity, my heart stopped. Without realizing, I was being thrown back in time. I relived the exact moment of impact.

As the headlights came toward us, my head jerked hard to my right as it had when we were hit that frigid evening. I realized I was staring out my own window, that we were not actually colliding, and that this was a flashback. I forced my heart to start beating again. I forced myself to breathe. Long, slow, deep breaths, in and out, with my eyes squeezed shut, until I could calmly say out loud, "Greg, I need to travel more at night to get over these feelings that I have. I did not realize I still have so much anxiety about traveling in the dark."

Although this was my first expedition into the night, it would not be my last flashback under such circumstances. That night I told myself if I conquered this episode, dealing with the apprehension and surviving to tell it, , I could conquer those to come.

But then, my greatest challenge is just that: demanding that I conquer, that I overcome, too much, too soon.

This fundraiser where many of our family and friends came to visit was what our family needed. We needed to see smiles and feel hugs. We needed to have an evening of change and enlightenment. We purposely arrived a little late because we didn't know how long I would last. Visiting for three hours was nothing short of a miracle. We were high off the spirit in the room. That night would also be the first time I gave a speech regarding my recovery. Was it emotional? The worst! I dislike being the center of attention, but this moment called for it. I had to personally thank these wonderful people for all their support over the last three months. I needed them to understand how grateful we were. This was important to me. There were many moments, like this one, where I didn't know how to get what I was feeling in my chest to come out in words, but I did my best. I felt strong until I looked at our children standing behind me. Then I faltered. My voice cracked as my throat filled up with thick emotion. Looking back at the crowd apologetically, I received several looks of "You can do this, Carey." That last statement would become my mantra for many more experiences to come.

—|—

As physical therapy sessions approached, I was excited and nervous all at once. April was the month I began my first voluntary torture showdown. Me versus induced pain. It was a crapshoot. Which one would win on those first visits? Having never experienced physical therapy before, I didn't know what to expect. I felt like a bag of bones petrified into the shape of a chair. Barely moving for over three months, muscle atrophy and inflexibility molded my frail, skinny frame.

Pure terror hit me when I imagined a stranger touching my ankles. Unable to bear the thought of multiple strangers working on me, I asked to be scheduled with one therapist only. Trust was essential in my participation.

There I was, sitting in my wheelchair, facing my therapist.

"What do you want to achieve from this therapy?" he asked.

"I want you to challenge and push me. I want to achieve, as closely as possible the activity level I had before I was hurt. I want to walk," I declared.

Then he examined my x-rays and listened to me go over the last three months of my life.

We both sighed.

"What is he going to do with me?" I speculated about my therapist.

Later, he shared that he also wondered, "What am I going to do with her?"

On that day he said, "See that cot butted up against the concrete wall? I want you to transfer from your wheelchair to the cot, then lay on your back."

"Flat?" I asked incredulously. My waist and pelvis were rebelling against the movement. Each part of my anatomy preferred the position it was in. None of my parts moved independently anymore.

"Flat," he repeated.

Pushing myself up and out of the wheelchair, leaving my knees bent and lowering myself down to my left side, I met the white cot with my shoulder and rolled to my back, sweating, profusely.

My "inducer of pain" pushed my knees to the mattress and my lower back revolted by awkwardly arching upward. "Oh Lord," I thought, "if this is the warmup, I am doomed."

"Roll to your stomach" was his next instruction.

My face went as blank as it would have if I did not understand what he was saying. "On my stomach?" I was flabbergasted. First off, my legs are in braces. I have not rolled anywhere in months. My pelvis and lower back pain are competing with each other, and he wants me to roll over?

"This is terrible, just terrible," I thought to myself as I rolled over. Amazed at my accomplishment. He then had the nerve to ask me to push up on my elbows. He measured the angle my torso was able to bend. I barely moved.

I am not liking physical therapy or this man. "Are we done yet?" I prayed out loud. Perspiration rolled down my spine as, plank-like, I rolled to my back. Then he announced he was going to stretch my ankles.

Like hell! Oh no. NO! NO! NO, NO, and NO! Do not even. Stay away. Do not touch. Do not even look. No.

"Okay," I heard myself say, timidly.

It took forever to remove my socks due to the fragility of my bones. We both stared at the damage. Scarred with an incredible amount of edema.

As I sat upright with my legs stretched out to the end of the cot, he said he needed to extend my ankles downward. "Pushing down on the top of your feet is the only way to regain movement."

I am panicked, stricken with fear. What if I throw up from the pain? I do not want to do this! I don't want to do this. "Let's do this," I state with false enthusiasm.

My eyes are squeezed shut. Hot pain flowed from my ankles up my lower legs at the lightest push. His hands shifted my feet downward even more. My right palm met the concrete wall with a smack, sweaty, with fingers splayed apart. "Dear God!" I screamed inside. The sound of my bones moving was nauseating. It was as if they were breaking apart all over again.

"I can do this. I can do this," I recited, to keep from sobbing. It was as if my ankles had been encased in old, crumbling concrete for a decade; and now they were being chiseled out, popping, grinding. My gasps engulfed me. I traveled back, relived the pain of that fateful night as I awoke in the car.

"This anguish cannot be as dreadful as that, could it?" I asked myself. My nose began to run with tears that I refused to let fall out of my tear ducts. A half sob, half laugh escaped me as my fingers clawed at the cold, beige wall. He held my stretched ankles down for what seemed like minutes. It was seconds.

"That's enough for today," he acknowledged.

Air rushed out of my lungs as I sighed with relief. My shoulders slumped and my head leaned against the wall as he strapped my braces back on my legs.

"How was your first visit?" he asked.

I threw a narrow side glance his direction, saying as much as if I had uttered the words aloud.

Leaving with sheets of exercises to perform at home, my list of goals running through my mind as my mom wheeled me to her truck. Determination set in; its long talons going deep inside me.

"Mom," I said. "Today, I stopped being a victim and became a survivor. I *will* recover from this."

My time sitting in a wheelchair had long since become mundane. Winter refused to release its grip, and I kept rolling around every room in the house trying to find adventure. Which is how I found myself sitting at the top of the stairs to the basement.

There it was, yet again—that attitude. I was worn out by the attitude I forced myself to maintain; my attention driven by thoughts of walking. Limbo—the greatest source of my frustration. I wanted to know if I would be able to stand again or whether I should accept that I must "roll" forever.

Sitting deep in thought, I worked myself into a frenzy. I got angry. I got angry because I couldn't stand. I got angry because of my inability to retrieve my own bowl from the cupboard. I got angry because I couldn't do anything without feeling pain.

I got angry because I couldn't visit my basement! Basement. There I was, still sitting at the top of the stairs, while at the bottom, leaning against the wall, were a pair of silver crutches, taunting me. Beckoning me.

Done with fragile ladylike words, I yelled "Oh fuck this!" at my empty house.

I slammed my palms on the arm rests of my wheelchair and declared, "I am done with sitting on my ass, relying on everyone to help me."

Rolling closer to the top step, it was clear I could not lower myself directly from my wheelchair to the floor. Locating my children's step stool, I placed it on the floor in front of the stairs, then proceeded in shifting myself to the stool, then to the floor, then to the top step.

I weighed nothing, but I had no strength and movement was painful. "What the hell. I've already been broken and survived. What could happen?"

Having used up four minutes moving about two feet from the stool to the steps, I realized it could take all day to master the stairs.

"What else do I have to do?" No answer.

Determination plunged me forward into the task. I started by placing my left foot, then my right onto the next stair, gingerly sliding my butt from one step to the next I reached the bottom. Before my momentum ran out, I leaned forward, grabbed the crutches, and hurled them as far as I could up the steps.

Looking back up the steps, it was like the hallway in a movie that grows longer the more the camera holds the shot. The stairs stretched up and up.

"How did I do that?" I asked. This talking out loud was getting to be a habit.

Whatever I did to come down, I must do again to climb up; in this direction, gravity was not working with me. My arms, back, and thighs were strained as I retreated back up the stairs, arriving safely to my metal chariot. Winded, covered in sweat, I glanced at the clock.

"It took me thirty minutes to do this?" I shouted.

So (forgive the pun) I was on a roll.

"I will stand today! I just have to figure out how."

Afraid to rest and risk losing my determination, I first reclaimed the crutches I had thrown up the stairs. Placing them across my lap, I rolled to the doorway and parked, facing the wall, assuming this was the safest tactic (relatively speaking).

"Lock the brakes of the chair," I told myself. "That way, if I fall, I'll either hit the wall or collapse back into the chair. Hopefully," my mind added.

Lifting the footrests, I placed each of my braced feet on the floor. These were my original black braces, which, by the way, were not manufactured for standing. Crutches were where they needed to be, so I began rocking back and forth in the chair so I could leverage myself upward. My fourth attempt landed me cheek-against-the-wall, gripping the door frame, scrambling to find a crutch before I crashed.

"This may be the most stupid decision I have ever made" crossed my mind and came out of my mouth. I did not have permission to do this, had never attempted this with supervision, and here I was doing it alone in my house. This was dumb.

"Since I'm already up, I shouldn't waste the opportunity."

The hardwood floor in the kitchen was a step away. Placing my weight on the crutches, my braces scraped against the oak wood as I dragged them forward. I looked across my kitchen and was dumbfounded by the view.

"My Lord! I am so tall!" I hadn't viewed anything from this level in months. I felt enormous. I loomed over the countertops. Deliriously happy, I broke into uncontrollable laughter. Coming from so deep inside, it made my belly ache. This was the first time I had a true, unforced laugh since our crash.

"I did it. I stood!" My voice had all the energy of a fist bump, without the fists.

Then my laughter turned into something else. Drooping on my crutches, shoulders sagged, body limp, I released deep, anguished sobs. I sucked in a deep gulp of air as each sobbing episode ended and another began. Then came more soundless sobbing as emotion engulfed me to the point that nothing came out. My eyelids seized shut. My mouth would not close. My face was contorted with the pain, grief, and fear I'd survived these past months. My shoulders were racked with each wave of emotion that came over me. I hung like a ragdoll on metal crutches.

I was able to release my pent-up grief. I opened my eyes. My shirt was wet from the river of tears that had been damned up, held back, contained. I was not sad. This was a healing cry.

I needed release. Staring down at the floor, I found a puddle of drool. I acknowledged how ridiculous I must have looked, drooling, and crying like an infant. That was what I call an ugly cry. Ugly, but much needed.

After wiping a grotesque amount of saliva off the floor, because all I would need now is to slip in it, I had to share this with my husband. Even though it was the middle of the day and he was at work, I had to share this with my confidante.

On the phone, I confessed my drama of the afternoon; my voice thick with feeling.

Greg remained quiet. I imagined him holding his head in his hands, thinking, "Woman, you are surely going to give me a heart attack," but he only had compassionate words for his wild wife.

I would say to anyone who planned something like this the same as I said to myself, "That was a foolish and hazardous decision. What were you thinking?"

It was not based on intellect. it was a decision based on emotion. I am stubborn and I do not regret it, and it was not the last time frustration won over common sense.

But it gave me hope. Strength can give you power, but hope can give you success.

My next adventure was all about satisfying my desire, not only to be more independent but to be able to have what I wanted when I wanted it. As with many mornings, I woke up impatient and agitated. Although my mind was becoming clearer as I decreased my narcotic use, I still could not guess the date or even the month. It seemed like it should be late April. I hoped it was. As I gained more clarity with each day, I felt my natural, active personality returning. Although my mind and imagination were getting more active, my muscles continued to atrophy, waiting for bones to take their own sweet time to heal.

I was able to wheel myself around and fix something to eat and drink. If I forgot to ask someone to get a plate or bowl down, I was stuck. My legs could not bear any weight, so standing up to get something out of the cabinet was impossible. On a cold, rainy spring morning, I wanted a cup of cappuccino to warm up my insides. I didn't have a grabber—one of those tools for elderly or disabled people to help grab things from the floor—but I was able to maneuver a butter knife into the coffee cup handle. Step one! As I looked up in the cabinet at how the cappuccino was out of reach, I wondered how I was going to accomplish this monumental task.

I tried and tried, but the knife was short of being able to scoot the container to the edge of the shelf. Plus, it was taking an extraordinary amount of time and energy out of my never-ending day, and I was getting quite frustrated. I started throwing things at the cappuccino container until it toppled over the ledge and *voilà!* I made myself a hot drink. A small, short-lived but rewarding endeavor.

One success, one frustration, another success, two more frustrations. I was living a mother-may-I game that most days took me two steps back, then another two steps back. But holding my cup of cappuccino in my hands felt a tremendous victory.

It almost didn't matter that an hour from now, I would again feel restless. Being aware of and able to endure this repetitive cycle was a huge part of my learning how to heal—impatient or not, restless or not, successful or not, it was about my resolve.

Chapter 6

Easter Mass

Whenever you find yourself doubting how far you can go,
just remember how far you have come. Remember everything
you have faced, all the battles you have won,
and all the fears you have overcome.

– N.R. Walker

Life was getting hard. Frustration, impatience, and pain had taken their toll on my mind, body, and spirit. I felt so dependent. Relying on others was not something I had experienced much in life. It was annoying.

The rest of my family had kept living their lives and had gotten back to normal; but when they came home, it was back to my world. I resented that I wasn't the mom or wife I wanted to be, or should have gotten to be during these times. I worried the kids would one day resent all of this—and me.

The truth is, they lit up my whole world when they came clamoring through the door after school. Usually, it was all smiling and a loud, "Hi, Mom!" Sometimes it was an exaggerated frown and grimaced face, then "Mom, guess what!" Either way, they were still looking to me and it was everything.

As my husband entered the house—a little more quietly and slowly than the kids—feeling his presence back home gave me relief. These two events were the highlight of my days and spurred me to keep clawing my way back to a place where I could function as a human being again.

There was one thing. One major thing, at least to me. I was feeling like a nuisance. A huge nuisance to everyone, including myself!

—|—

Our situation had me unsettled in every way possible. Greg would let me know when I was becoming grouchy. Grouchy meant it was affecting the moods of our family. I would talk to myself, trying to find a place of calm. Greg was my coach and my motivator when I found myself struggling. His natural ability to guide people was (and is) amazing, and here he was putting his business skills as a life coach to use on his wife. He pushed me enough but not too much. He held me when I needed to release the heaviness. But he did not coddle me.

Knowing me better than anyone, he knew coddling was not what I needed. That would not have helped me with my fight.

I could feel it was taking its toll on him. I could see the weight of it. He continually reminded me he had strong shoulders; he could handle this. I never doubted his love or commitment, but this recovery was going to be longer than either of us had ever imagined.

There were no raging fights between us, no anger. When emotions got heated, we would bring each other back to the place where we felt connected again, reminding each other how hard we had fought to blend our families as one family and not two; and we were going to continue that fight through this latest, toughest challenge.

Deep, emotional conversations were a norm. I kept hitting barriers, but I was tenacious! It was clear I was not going back to work any time in the near future; and having spent the prior year back at college, our savings were depleted. Medical bills were arriving in our mailbox by the tens of thousands. Medical pay from our auto insurance had been intercepted by the hospitals to pay for my care. When I heard the word "subrogation" for the first time in my life, it sent me over the edge. Any cash settlement we received would be taken and split between the health insurance, medical care, and our attorneys.

It all felt wrong—like I had done something wrong. My life was in complete upheaval. My family was in pain; I was disabled; and we were all paying the physical, emotional, and now financial price.

I asked out loud, "How much more? How much more can our family take and not crumble from the pressure?"

That question took me a few days to absorb before I could collect myself enough to find my grit again. My pep talk consisted of this: "Life happens, Carey. Bad things happen to good people every day. Make a choice. Right now. How are you going to handle this?"

Easter was late that year, April 24th. Our priest suggested that I wait to come to church until my pain lessened and I became more mobile. Unable to drive or attend many of my family's activities, but unable to stand being cooped up any longer, I asked my husband to take me to mass. Rolling me into church, I could feel warm eyes on me. Although welcome, I felt small in that wheelchair, stripped of my independence. Dragging my bottom from the chair to the hard, wooden bench, I cringed. I had forgotten to bring a seat cushion. Weighing around 110 pounds, there was not much padding for my sore tailbone that I had been relentlessly abusing for months. One of our daughters gave me her coat to ease my discomfort and stop the grinding sound that came from my constant fidgeting.

With that taken care of, my ankles started talking to me, and before long they were barking. By the time we got to communion, they were howling. Since they are elevated most of the day to relieve the pressure of my injuries, an hour of hanging down caused deep aches and a pounding each time my heart took a beat. I sat on the right side of church, in the front row, at the end of the pew, farthest from the center aisle. I had not heard or absorbed a single word of mass since entering the church. Concentrating on increasing my comfort and berating myself for being impatient with my progress, I lost the purpose of attending mass with my family.

I knew Easter Mass was a tad longer than a normal Sunday devotion. Admitting silently that this was not one of my best ideas, communion commenced, meaning it was close to ending.

Keeping my head down as parishioners received the Eucharist, I felt the first soft touch on my right shoulder. Gently smiling, I covered this man's hand and nodded thank you. Lacing my fingers together, I laid my clasped hands in my lap as another hand gingerly touched my shoulder as they passed by me, another patting, another squeezing, another caressing, another and another and another.

Each one of these wonderful angels spoke volumes to me as they moved past. No words. Just touches. Soft, compassionate, reassuring touches on my shoulder. This was not sorrow or pity for what had happened to me. This was normal people being sent as angels to comfort. One hot tear fell from the corner of my right eye and then one more. As more parishioners compassionately moved past me, more tears fell. I could not lift my eyes for fear of an emotional collapse. So many hands that I could not count, touched first my shoulder and then my heart.

With nothing to wipe my eyes, I sat there, slightly bent, tears dripping from the contours of my face to the fabric of my pants, as the line moved forward. My face was hot. Silent sobs racked my chest as I kept them from escaping. Unable to hide what was transpiring within me, my soaked eyelashes laid on my cheeks for the remainder of the hour.

That day, sitting miserably on a hard wooden church pew, I was reminded by the innumerable touches on my shoulder that life is to be lived gratefully and selflessly. I was reminded that spiritual grace and gratitude are not to be taken out for holidays or when tragedy pounds on our doors. I found solace knowing that even though I had heard none of the words recited from scripture, God told me everything I needed to hear, transmitted through touch.

It is said that, if angels exist, they have wings and halos above their heads, that they show themselves when we reach so deeply within ourselves that we touch a place we never knew we even had.

I see angels every day—especially on that day, with my head bent and tears clouding my sight, I saw angels all around me.

Chapter 7

Resolve

If you fall off your horse, get back in the saddle.

I clung to this common quote, recited by my mother and many before her, hearing it in my mind with each "tumble and spill" that tested my resolve. I lived it, both literally and figuratively. I grew up riding horses and, as a child, was thrown from my saddle a couple of times. My father ordered me to get back on my horse after a fall. I remember staring at him with a look of dismay, then pouting angrily as I put one foot in the stirrup, grabbed the reins, and headed back to the barn. I got back in the saddle but I was angry about it.

As a normal adolescent, I never admitted my parents were right about anything. Now as an adult, it's clear that parents have a certain responsibility to leverage youthful experiences, turning them into learning moments. Such lessons are for the betterment of our children. We hope that, at those junctures in our children's lives, the words of wisdom will be there for them to use. We aspire that they may even be able to smile as they repeat the words said to them in their younger years and that they exclaim, "Oh my, I sound like my mom/dad!"

This quote has been my chant as I have had to *get back on that horse* several times during this recovery. My trauma surgeon informed me in no uncertain terms that I could stay in a hospital bed, in my living room, and live in a wheelchair, or...I could conquer my anxiety, work long and hard, all the while knowing my body might fail.

But what if I succeeded?

Choosing to get back in that saddle was the only option for me. I am fortunate that is my natural response. Whether it comes from deep within me or from my upbringing, I do not care. Succeeding requires resolve. I realized knowing how to ride was not enough. I had to know how to fall. There is an art to keeping a horse between you and the ground. There is a discipline to recovering. I must always be thinking ahead. Preparation is key. Sometimes I have to take a risk by sitting in that saddle and saying, "Well, let's see what happens."

Physically, I am not able to carry out activities as I would have before my injuries; however, I have learned great patience and creativity. Analyzing the situation and adapting have been my greatest achievements. The lessons I have cultivated from my tragedy are invaluable. I have an improved sense of myself and more empathy for others because of it.

As months slipped by, my physical therapist noticed my pelvis was not moving correctly. Knowing we had a farm with horses, he suggested equine therapy. I had a young horse named "Jack" and knew we could trust him to do the job. He stands at fourteen-point-two hands and is a perfect gentleman with me.

"How am I supposed to get in the saddle?" I asked. I had begun to walk ever so slowly with a walker, but mounting a horse? My physical therapist said that was for me to figure out.

"Come here, babe" Greg picked me up and sat me on the tailgate of the truck. "Grab Jack's halter."

I did and I pulled Jack's muzzle close to my cheek. "Jack, we need to talk," I said. "I'm a bit fragile. My legs hurt terribly. I need you to be gentle and patient with me. Don't do anything crazy, *please.*"

With Greg helping to stabilize me on the tailgate of our truck, I was able to gingerly, awkwardly, slide onto Jack's back, then Greg led us into our round pen. I walked Jack in a circle. My physical therapist instructed me to ride bareback so I could concentrate on allowing my hips to move in synchronization with Jack's strides. My legs hung over his sides. The reins in my hands, I prayed this would not only help me move better but that he also would obey my weak leg commands.

With sheer determination, I willed my mind and body to relax. I became one with my horse. I went back to a place of calm that I always felt, even as a child, when I was astride my horse's back, transmitting messages to him through my thoughts and body.

I could feel something was not right. There, bareback, moving with Jack, I realized that the screws in my pubic bone were a tad too long. I vowed to discuss this with my surgeon, even though I knew this would lead to another pelvic surgery. Some things need to be adjusted.

As I continued to move with Jack, I felt such gratitude because I was able to share this moment, with Greg and also my daughter Olivia, who was capturing it on video so I could look back and remember this momentous time in my life. Greg looked at me with relief, pride, and an enormous amount of love. Having been scared silly that I would never be able to ride again, an overwhelming feeling of accomplishment washed over me. I felt elation, sorrow, and appreciation, all rising up out of my chest, into my throat. I wanted to shout! Greg, Olivia, and I were smiling from ear to ear.

Moments like those gave me hope that I could find fulfillment in my "new normal."

Right then, it was enough. I was rewarded by being back on a horse, feeling the movement and knowing I was making progress. I accepted that riding Jack had replenished my spirit and strengthened my resolve to take on the next challenge.

I do believe challenges are put in our path so we can make choices about who we want to be and what we want out of lives.

—|—

Most of us have some sort of extended family. Although we may not get to spend much time with them, we know they will always step up to the plate when we are in need. Greg and I had a long list of people that we considered extended family. It kept growing! Whole communities supported us through my recovery. Their actions confirmed our faith in each other and our communal ability to rally when one of our members is down.

—|—

Nearly seven months had passed since our collision. I had already completed, I believe, five surgeries on my pelvis and bilateral ankles combined. A few weeks prior, I had learned to take my first steps using a walker and had progressed to using a walker with wheels! What was equally exciting was that I put on a pair of shoes for the first time in six months! The ominous wheelchair was still in my life, but it was no longer my source of mobility.

It was the time of year for the Crawford County Fair. Knowing my wheelchair would not endure the ruts and ridges of a fair, and still dedicated to not allowing my condition to dictate the activities of our family, I had to figure out how we could all participate. The kids had to take care of their livestock animals and have some fun. Greg and I also needed a "pick me up" and a little socializing ourselves.

I decided I could endure two trips a day to the swine barn sitting on my blue walker with wheels, as long as the kids took turns pushing me. If I recall correctly, it was 117 degrees that July. Maybe I'm exaggerating here, but it seems the heat rises when the county fair begins. The extreme heat did not help my already massively swollen ankles. Nevertheless, we endured, had fun, and all week our family received well wishes, hugs, and sincere compassion from all who knew us. And there was one moment that took the cake.

It was at Saturday's livestock sale. I sat next to the sale ring waiting for our kids to emerge one by one with their animals.

Olivia and Mackenzie won the top two awards in the swine division. We were all delighted!

As Olivia walked the ring with her pig, I had one camera in my left hand taking a video and another camera in my right-hand snapping photos. I was being a "mom" and mouthing for her to "smile and look at the crowd" when I heard the auctioneer announce she had set a record.

"What?" I had been so busy juggling my cameras and insisting my daughter keep a smile on her face that I had not heard a single word the auctioneer had said. Both cameras stopped following my daughter as I turned my head to the right to look at the crowd. There were a lot of people sitting in those bleachers, but I did not see a single face as I slowly took in what our wonderful community had done. Then I searched until I found my husband, leaning against a wall with his hands stuck deep in his pockets. His eyes were swimming with unshed tears, which confirmed what I thought had transpired. Our community family had come together and bid the sale price of Olivia's grand champion hog to a new high. It set a fair sale record. I held his stare so long that he walked over, knelt beside me, wiped the tears from my cheeks with his calloused knuckles and smiled.

"These are good people, Carey," he said.

"Indeed, they are," I agreed.

Olivia's hog brought seventeen dollars a pound on that hot, humid day. My daughter had no trouble keeping a smile from taking over her entire face. To top it off, the hog was donated back to be auctioned off, this time to help with medical expenses! I made a feeble attempt to focus on the rest of the sale, but it was futile. Leaving the show pavilion, an acquaintance said in earnest, "Carey, I believe this Crawford County Fair is the start to a better second half of this year." I believed that with all my heart.

Looking back, I am not sure how I was able to attend that fair or endure the pain it cost me, but I would not have traded that moment for one pain-free day. It was another turning point, the boost our family needed but never would have asked for. That is what friends do best. We couldn't have been prouder of being part of such a giving community.

I realized at that point that the standards I set for myself are the measure of my dedication to recover. I respect myself too much to expect anything less than my best effort. My family is expecting my best effort, as well. The standards I expect of others must be the same standards I follow. No one supports a hypocrite. When I wonder how much more I can handle or if walking again is worth the effort, I remember this measure of commitment and know that I will continually rededicate myself to my best efforts.

Chapter 8

Believe

*Do not pray for an easy life, pray for the strength
to endure a difficult one.*

— Bruce Lee

*Pain has a way of tearing you down to your most
vulnerable self. It can be physical, mental, or emotional
pain. When it hits, it usually hits hard, slowly slithering
its way into your body or mind and then slamming you
to your very core.*

When my husband arrived home to find a new inspirational
quote on the wall, he could positively assume his wife needed
extra motivation. This first year of recovery was a toss-up be-
tween physical, mental, and emotional pain. I experienced all
three at once.

My traumatic arthritis was in "end stage." The nerve dam-
age I suffered had grown to be all-consuming. Flare-ups from
either were normal. Some days, no hot whirlpool bath, ice
packs, or pleading could ease the deep-seated ache that bore
its way into my bones.

So, to cope, I reverted to a technique I had used successfully before. A form of meditation, I would guess. I recited quotes over and over and over. I had them everywhere. On my walls, in my closet, in my drawers, on my phone. Everywhere, a reminder of how fortunate I was and that I will always endure and defeat what is challenging me.

Literally speaking, I must see the quote to remind myself to concentrate. Then I recite it in my head, again and again. When the pain is at its worst, it's not enough to read the words. I have to say them out loud. I must say them with conviction! "I WILL BE OKAY!" It does not work unless I strip everything away, then convince my whole heart, mind, and soul into *believing it.*

But sometimes—and there were times—the pain engulfed me to the point that I could only whisper, "God, please grant me the strength to keep fighting." Then when the pain threatened to pull me into its darkness, I'd let my tears fall, unashamed, because when one cannot speak, God observes tears as prayers, too. At that point in time, I had a perfect record of surviving my worst days. And I willed myself to *keep fighting!*

The point is that all pain is pain. Pain hurts. Pain tears us down. We must find our inspiration to fight through the challenges in our lives from any source we can. If we do not have support, we must inspire ourselves. How well we do something is determined by our attitude. We can lie down and let pain devour us, or we can choose to make peace with our situation and fight for our lives.

I bare my soul here, not only to heal but to let others living in pain know that I understand and I believe surviving it is possible. I say to all those in pain—lean into the pain, believe past the pain. Hear my truth, my words: "Believe" in surviving.

I am still here.

Each person's version of pain and surviving may look different from mine, but the steps to overcoming it are the same. There are days that surviving is the best that I can do; other days, I can thrive. Those thriving days are the ones that I cherish and tuck away to keep me humble and motivated. I live for the feeling of those days.

Chapter 9

Seriously?

I am not what happened to me. I am what I choose to become.

– Carl Gustav Jung

I am not exaggerating when I say that I was sent home from the hospital with a plethora of narcotics. There were so many, Greg produced a spreadsheet to keep track. Every two hours, I would swallow pills that sucked me back into some world where I and a few other characters lived.

Back in real life, my family members would pass by my living-room bedside in a blur, at least through my eyes. No one was moving fast. That's what happens to perceptions when taking Oxycontin, Percocet, Norco, and on and on.

For three months, I existed in this state of delirium. Most of the memories that were created around me disappeared as the next round of pills hit my stomach. Having no idea of the conversations I had with my children or husband made me lonely. It was as if they were here, but I wasn't, or I was and they weren't.

At every step of the way, I took my recovery very seriously. However, many months after decreasing the pain meds, my family disclosed versions of adventures of which, I was the only participant. My objections, surprise, denials were all met with their amused expressions. Obviously, this was out of character for me, although engaging for my audience.

Our four children were watching over me one day when, evidently, it must have been around lunchtime. Or maybe I speculated it was lunchtime.

"Who ate my sandwich?" I asked. My children stood dumbfounded in silence. "Which one of you stole my sandwich?" I asserted again.

"I don't think you had a sandwich, Mom," one of my children answered.

"I know one of you took it. You need to give it back," I said with frustration.

This story doesn't have an ending that I know of (I've never asked), but it does have its humorous side. They may have produced another sandwich to satisfy my distress over the one that was missing, feigned one; but my mind probably wandered off to attend to another adventure.

They have retold this story more than a few times in my presence. I sit by, in disbelief, but I do snicker.

There is also another episode of me petting an imaginary cat in our living room. As I lay in my bed, one of the kids caught me making an odd motion over my lap.

"Mom, what are you doing?"

"Petting a cat," I stated.

"Whose cat?" our child asked.

"Our cat!" I said. Never mind that we didn't have a cat.

I have always felt I had control of myself and my memories, so I still shake my head when I can't find even a vague recollection of these episodes. That said, I vividly recall Drew running through the house yelling at our other children not to go into the living room because "Mom's poopin'!"

When my children finish reliving these comedies, I inquire of them, "What is the moral of this story, kids?" There is some shrugging of shoulders, blank stares.

I burst out, "Don't Do Drugs!!!" Joking, yet serious, there must be a moral, right?

—|—

Our motor vehicle crash report is a public document. Anyone can view it via the internet. However, I am the one who relives the emotions while reading about my own tragedy on a piece of paper.

I spent an hour pouring over it, rereading it again and again, unsure about what I wanted to believe, piecing together facts that I could not draw out from my own recollection. It had much more of an effect on me than I had anticipated. I came across it innocently as I was rifling through our "crash" folder looking for my surgeon's phone number. I gently removed it. Nine months into recovery, I read through the entire document.

I confirmed by reading that four vehicles were involved, not the two cars I recalled. A section at the bottom of the page shows, in heavy black circles, the damage to the car I was driving that frosty evening. One section is not circled: the trunk lid. That was the only part of the car that did not receive damage that night.

I turned the page and read that a full-size pickup truck had hit us. I viewed the other drivers' names that were involved. I wondered about them. How are they doing now? How did they react? Olivia's and Mackenzie's names are printed in black and white as victims. My chest tightened at the bold type that listed their names, address, birth dates, sex, numbers that indicate which seat they were in. More numbers illustrated which air bag deployed, if anyone was ejected or transported elsewhere. Seeing their ages, ten and twelve, written down was a stab in my heart. They were too young to have been forced to survive and learn to thrive through a hardship of such magnitude.

Reading, I asked myself if they, at any time, thought we might die? I wondered if they would view life differently; and I know intuitively that as they mature, this experience will stay inside them in some form, along with the trauma of my recovery and what we have all experienced after the collision.

Then I read, "Statements from both drivers and witnesses."

My statement? Could I give a statement? When? Did I give them the details while I was still trapped in the car or was I in the ambulance? Perhaps when I was in the hospital. I don't recall giving any statement. I read the document to learn what I had to report.

"We were headed east into Cuba. I told the girls *he* was on the wrong side of the highway."

The other drivers' statements were the same as mine: The pickup was driving in the wrong lane. Witness accounts noted that the driver was traveling at a high rate of speed (in excess of eighty-five mph) as the pickup passed them around corners and up hills.

I tried to picture this through others' eyes, driving in the dark on that December evening, viewing it from their perspective. It's terrifying. They remembered all of it. I had to piece it together, filling in the holes in my memory, still trying to make sense of the statements.

Witnesses stated:

"He tapped his brakes."

"He fishtailed."

"As I came over the hill, lights were everywhere."

"Car parts were falling from the air when I drove up."

When I read our girls' statements, my chest ached from being so tight. I did not realize they would take a minor's statement.

"I saw sparks fly, and I saw the other car hit the truck and trailer in front of us. I heard Mom scream, 'Oh my God.'" Mackenzie's statement.

I gasped. There was no room in my chest. Air solidified in my lungs, like blocks of ice, unyielding, unwilling to allow breath in or out. I did not remember the trailer but, yes, I distinctly remember screaming "Oh, my God!" I screamed it so loud the residents in town could have heard it, at least that is the way it felt.

"We were driving and, all of the sudden, Mom yelled and all the lights went out." Olivia's statement.

Reading their words hurled me right back in that car, and I felt everything as if it had happened seconds before. Their reality tore at the thick scab that had grown over my hysterical wounds. Sobs rose up and out of my body before I could stop them, like a kitchen faucet had been turned on; the warm tears cascaded down my face, onto my collapsed chest. It was the girls' pain that hit me the hardest. I couldn't handle their pain.

I asked whoever would listen if this rawness I felt in my chest would ever ease. I asked if I would ever be able to think or speak of this time without it ripping my chest open.

I read the last paragraph, a closing assessment of what had occurred. Many, many times over the past nine months, I questioned myself, "Had I done anything to help avoid the collision, to save our children?"

I would have done anything, right? This report confirmed that, indeed, I did try to help us.

"Driver Two took evasive action to the right, running off the right side of the road, to avoid Vehicle One. Vehicle Two traveled off the south side of Route ZZ and struck a tree before coming to a rest in the south ditch, facing west."

It may have been instinct for me to jerk to the right, and I am forever grateful that I did. Because of that, even though the truck hit us head on, the impact was on my side of the car. The truck stopped spinning as it slammed into my driver-side door. This spared Mackenzie in the front seat from the head-on collision and Olivia in the left passenger back seat from a second impact.

I can release the horrible fear that I hadn't done something I should have, could have done. I felt relief flowing over me, knowing I did all that I could.

After returning from work that evening, Greg sat with me as I told the story about my impassioned afternoon. I sobbed again, reliving the details. Once I finished, he looked at me, apologetically and sympathetically, then held my hands.

He stated, looking into my eyes, "Carey, that is the third time you have read that crash report."

I sat in silence, mouth gaping. "What? You mean, we have done this before? We've had this same conversation?" I asked in awe.

A simple nod, yes.

I have poured over these details, reliving this, feeling my children's pain three times?

"Did I react this way the other two times? Did my heart clench like this each time I read the report?"

"Yes, mostly. You are clearer now, but it has had the same effect. I leave it where it is because it seems like you need to keep going over everything. Like you say, you need to put the pieces of the puzzle together."

"How many more memories have I lost?" I asked him in a daze. "I feel betrayed by my own mind, Greg."

"Maybe your mind was doing you a favor," he offered.

I stopped thinking and realized, "Yes, it is possible that my mind was doing me a favor. It is conceivable that I am only able to absorb this, nine months after the collision. Maybe I couldn't handle it before now." Well, maybe my subconscious is smarter than I give it credit for. I went on. "You sat quietly, patiently listening to me mourn over the same details three times. You let me finish each time?"

A small wink. "It's what you needed," he whispered and kissed me on my lips.

My chest relaxed. Air flowed freely into my lungs; heaviness left my body as if fog were being burned off by the morning sun. This time my tears were for the man God had sent to me, who has been unwavering in his support of my many and long recoveries.

As another season passes and I turn the page to a new month, I accept that not knowing everything may not be as great of an annoyance as I had previously thought. What I need to know about the past is that no matter what has happened, it has all worked to bring us to this juncture and will continue to guide us into the unpredictable future.

Chapter 10

Attitude

And once the storm is over, you won't remember
how you made it through, how you managed to survive.
You won't even be sure, whether the storm is really over.
But one thing is certain. When you come out of the storm,
you won't be the same person who walked in.
That's what this storm's all about.

— Haruki Murakami

A serious car collision changed our family. In looking at us dispassionately, I'd say we have done a good job of not letting it define who we are in a negative way. Times have been hard, each wave of challenges threatening to drown us. They are gradually receding.

The most gratifying aspect is that we battled each challenge together, refusing to allow life's circumstances to rip our family apart. Greg and I were passionate about this. We worked hard to make our family feel as one and we would not allow another's decision to steal that from us.

Before the tragedy, our lives were rushed. Working overtime, carting kids to practices and events, many of those overlapping each other. Hugs and kisses were quick as I hurried one child out the car door to run the other child across town, then to run the three errands I needed before the first one had to be picked up again. Uniforms to wash, dinner to cook, homework that I did not understand myself. Thinking back, I recall hearing myself talk about all the tasks that had to be done. I don't remember ever thinking of them as tasks that I had the honor of doing. I did not resent them, but there were so many to be done with so little time, I did not feel privileged to do them.

My husband and I would see each other in passing, shouting encouragement to each other. Our life was happy, but I desired more quality time with those I loved. I begged myself to find a way to slow down, to be able to hold my children's hands while strolling, not dragging them along because they were walking too slow. I wanted to flirt with my husband and maybe take a few hours for myself, doing some hobby that I had not had time to think about yet. I wanted time to look at life, remember, and enjoy it.

Now then, let's be clear. I had asked myself to figure out how to make my life slow down, not come to a complete halt.

Our collision handed to me what I could not accomplish on my own in a painful package. It's not exactly how I would have done it; but then, as I stated earlier, perhaps I was not specific enough in my prayers.

When I began to recover and was able to start tending to my family again, everything I took for granted pre-collision came into vivid focus. I had never felt anything so clearly in my life, and I discovered it was a clarity I had been searching for over many years. It took a speeding truck breaking my body to pieces to give me what I desired. How selfish of me. How indebted I am because of it.

I had been a glass-half-full kind of gal instead of a glass-half-empty. Now I'm asking, what if the glass is bigger than it needs to be? That is how my perception has changed.

In my present, I can watch my kids in all their activities with nothing on my mind except them, and I can embed every moment into my forever memory. I don't care or think about what else I should be doing or if someone else wants my attention. My children have all of me. I hold each gaze of each child and smile, just because.

I am grateful hearing my children heckle each other. I am happy to see their pouts after being told, "No." I cherish every smile, sitting in the stands of their events, admiring each performance. I am even grateful (this is hard to believe, but true) I can sit through middle school choir concerts.

Ten years and many surgeries later, our children are graduated from high school and making plans of their own. When my children were born, I felt like we had all the time in the world because the age of eighteen seemed so far away. Since the accident, I have found myself traveling back to those days when the kids were young and freezing moments so that I may cherish them more intently. I feel as if these past ten years, since our world was changed so drastically, was a blink in our timeline. Our children have and always will be my "why." They are the reason I continued to fight so hard to become whole again. They are the reason I continue to fight today! I don't want to miss a thing by giving up on life.

I realize now how much time I had spent viewing others' lives and ask, as I view my own, if everything seems as dramatic and urgent as it did before my crash. I say "No," which allows me to fall back onto a tried-and-true motto: KISS—Keep It Simple, Stupid. What had been words are now part of my daily implementation plan. It is easy, if I continue making the effort to keep it so.

Life is wonderful. There is kindness. There is simplicity—but I must choose to view it as such.

Stealing a quote from Mr. Abraham Lincoln, I invite you, my reader, to share this ponderous notion:

> *We can complain because rose bushes have thorns*
> *or rejoice because thorn bushes have roses.*

It is our choice.

The first year of recovery, I was grieving a death. I went through all the stages of grief, as if I had lost someone. I wondered when my heart would heal. I had to dig down to a place so deep inside of me, I worried I might not find my way back.

Living in this redefined and unsettling world, I questioned whether peace, calm, and a new normal would ever come. I asked if there would come a time when I felt like I had a greater purpose beyond healing. The answers were not immediately forthcoming.

However, it is true. I did find that the grieving process began to decline after the first year, but only because I grabbed on, deciding I was going to live instead of allowing grief, pain, and loss to control me or my family.

All those stages during healing, when I could focus on one hour at a time, transformed into whole days. I lived with an incessant question, "Am I going to be okay?" I do not recall intentionally or purposely asking this, yet it managed to work its way into my thoughts. I spoke with God each day, never asking why, only asking that same boomerang question, "Am I going to be okay?" Once I shouted out loud, "Say something!"

I don't agree with those who say that God wants us to let it all be in His hands. What I got from Him instead was "Take responsibility. Listen to your words and go do something wonderful with them. Take action with your life knowing I am by your side."

I approached the first anniversary of our crash with mixed feelings. Knowing it was coming, I had tried to anticipate which emotions might come over me to somehow prepare myself. Normally, being a low-key person, I don't allow emotions to overwhelm me, except on occasion. How would I react to this day that held a whole year of constant pain, anxiety, deep conversations, and "barely there" memories, all jumbled inside of me?

Then it happened. The anniversary date, December 29th. I felt something lift, some heaviness released my burdened spirit. For the previous twelve months, I had been grieving for a life that was gone. I was grieving for myself. I was grieving for a life that I would never have again. Grieving for time lost with my children, memories that would never make it to a permanent place in my mind. And especially, the pain that our family endured.

How did we make it through all of this? How did I? By supporting each other. Repeatedly. As one of us would stumble, another would lift the other up. We chose *our attitudes.* Every day. We still choose, because this is our life.

I believe the grief, acceptance, and grit that has always been inside of me have healed me, making me who I am today. It is my hope that our children view those same qualities in themselves. The crash *has* changed us. It has molded us into our future selves and how we will respond to new challenges. Our children can defy odds they never thought they could because they have already defied the most difficult challenge they have ever faced. And they survived!

One more big thing, one integral aspect of my first year of healing that spurred me on: *Forgiveness.*

This man made a terrible choice one Wednesday evening. He chose to drive under the influence. He changed my life and lost his. He did not slip into his truck in the frigid darkness and set out to hurt me, but he left me with the consequences of his choice.

How could I forgive him?

This is the one time in my life where I chose to be selfish. Forgiveness is for me. It brings me peace. A calmness. Without this, I would be bound by anger and bitterness. I know, undoubtedly, that I would not have healed physically, mentally, and emotionally without it. And not without strengthening my relationship with God.

We are products of our past, but that does not mean we have to be prisoners of it. Many people are driven by resentment and anger. They hold on to the hurt for comfort because releasing it through forgiveness seems more difficult. Resentment always hurts us more than the person we are resentful of; and, in my case, other than in my dreams, my offender is not here for me to confront.

I've learned that whatever has hurt me in the past cannot continue to hurt me unless I allow it! The past is that—something that has passed. Nothing will change it. The best I can do is learn from it, apply what I learned to my future, and then: Let. It. Go.

I choose forgiveness for me. If my life did not have meaning, did not have purpose, I would not have been able to bear that first year of recovery. Life without purpose is the greatest of all tragedies.

One man changed my life with a single choice. Now and forever, it is my turn to choose how I am going to react to it.

Every single day, life will throw things at us that we cannot control. But we get to wake up and we get to choose how we are going to react to it.

– Carey Portell

What choice will you make?

Epilogue

This story is about an event, a choice, that changed lives in an instant. It focuses on my recovery and what it took to get through the first year after the crash. The collision that took place on December 29, 2010, altered how our family came together during the worst of times. During the years since the collision, we have been able to survive and thrive, heal and recover, and experience normal transitions, like finishing school and going off to college.

I deliberately kept references to our four children out of this book as much as possible. This epilogue is an opportunity for them to share their insights about what they learned from this experience. Their words speak eloquently to the united courage, determination, and resilience—along with the laughter—that got us through that first year. We have grown and learned from this challenge, even while we faced it head on!

Hayley
That night, though terrible, led me and my family to many different realizations. It reminded us that, although we are only a family by marriage, the bonds and love we have for each other are as strong as blood. Most importantly, the accident taught me that every moment

is precious and to never take your family for granted. The effects of the crash on each one of us were different. Whether extreme, mild, emotional, or physical, it changed us, and I can only hope that it was for the better.

Olivia

I felt our experience made me mature quicker than my friends. I helped my younger brother get ready for school each morning while Greg took care of my mom before he left for work. Distracted driving is causing people pain all over the world. People need to take charge and make a difference. Our family has experienced a trauma that most families do not and there are many things we can do to stop it. If anybody has lost anyone they loved from a drunk-driving crash, wouldn't they do anything to prevent that from happening to someone else? The littlest choices can have the biggest outcomes.

Mackenzie

That night changed everything for me. It made me look at things differently. It made me appreciate things more, like my family, and how little I knew about my stepmom and sister. That crash bonded our relationship like nothing else ever could have. No one else will ever have the same feeling and understanding about that night that we have.

Drew

As a child, when I heard my mom and sisters had been hurt in a crash, I didn't want to believe it. I couldn't eat for days or stop thinking about it. This event has changed the way I see my life. I am more grateful for those who are close to me, especially my family.

Made in the USA
Las Vegas, NV
13 March 2023

68973969R00075